COMMISSIONED

Be Brilliant!!

COMMISSIONED

AZURE ANTOINETTE

(al·chem·ik)
press

Published by Aalchemik Press
www.aalchemikpress.com
.
Library of Congress Cataloging-in-Publication data on file.

Book Design by Kathy Kikkert

Printed in the United States of America

To Veronica & Susana

Thank you for showing me how
to love magic.
For taking a pause in life to find
beauty in the illusion.
You were right, it's beautiful.

You two confirm my belief in
alchemy.
Thank you for being the kind of
humans I can't live without.

Here is to Brilliance, Here is to
the word yes, and summers in
Manhattan, hailing cabs that
may never stop to pick us up.

CONTENTS

»»» EDITOR'S NOTE

There's a job I secretly covet, that you won't see on my resume. I do it when I'm reading the menu at a restaurant, when I'm walking down the streets of New York City and scanning the signs of store fronts, and when I was a kid, I even did it sitting in the church pew, my little pencil marking up the service bulletin. Editing. I was born to be a copy editor of the world.

When Azure asked me to be the editor of Commissioned, I didn't think about my many other commitments, or whether I had the right experience to edit a book. I just said "yes." Saying "no" wasn't an option to the woman I call the Maya Angelou of my generation. Little did I know that this project would be a luscious testimonial to the power of saying "yes."

Nor did I know back in March 2011, when I tweeted into the universe in search of a partner poet for She's the First, that I would find a woman who would so profoundly change my life. And I am just one of many in the ever-expanding ripple effect of her work in New York City. It was the best tweet I ever sent. Azure would teach me that poetry was not meant to be shelved in libraries with Emily Dickinson and Robert Frost. It is meant to be spoken, lived, and once in a while, to even break the rules of grammar.

—*Tammy Tibbetts*

» » FOREWORD

The best thing my mother ever did for me was a thing she did before she ever knew my name.

Before my father carted the bassinet through the doorway of a new upstairs bedroom, walls still heavy with layers of wet lavender paint. Before they stayed up at night, gazing at the ceiling fan and humming to the thought of sweet baby girls hands. & baby girl feet.

My mother tells me it was the book of Matthew.

Matthew was the place she bartered with God for a blessing. Said a short prayer, pulled open the book while she closed her own eyes, and placed her finger down to random words on the page. She was demanding Direction and she found Matthew. 10:10.

"take no bag for the journey, or extra tunic, or sandals or a staff; for the worker is worth his keep." (NIV)

Twenty-One words later and she was quitting her job. Breaking off a marriage. Packing a toothbrush. And travelling across country to finally breathe life into a Life all hers. & find the others. The others who travel through this world with little more than a backpack because God has blessed their life with the kind of coating He uses to tint the angels' wings.

They are out there.

As scattered but brilliant as the hooks of the vain queen Cassiopeia's throne sitting in the sky.

And when you find these people--the ones who are living, fleshy personifications of a Steve Jobs' quote--you keep them closer. Closer than friends. Closer than enemies. Close enough to let them breathe down your neck and make you uncomfortable enough to know that, if you both met eyes in the moment, something would be said among pupils and shades of blue: It is time for you to be moving. Going. Pushing off, no matter how scared it makes you.

And so you listen.

And you listen to their poetry on floors of Brooklyn apartments that can barely raise up their hands to say, "Lived in, I am lived in." No, those Poet-holding apartments in Brooklyn will always be jealous of the Other Lovers in that poet's life: the road. LAX. Coffee shops. Libraries where Dickinson falls off the shelves like manna.

You listen to their poetry with clam chowder cradled in your hands, probably scraped from the sides of a pot poured four hours ago. And you choose to believe in God. & other things. In people who have put their stakes in the Grounds of Poetry-- like the days when Barnum used to roll through town-- but have walked away from pen & page to breathe life into a Life all their own.

Then, only then, will a poem fully disarm us. & make words as sacred as "Fall on your knees/ Oh hear the angel's voices" be the kind of things we think to carry on the roads where we've been promised nothing just as much as everything.

Azure & I -- we're no strangers to a space where Change Makers & Shakers sit beside Artists in sandboxes until the sun sets down behind a hill. Where worlds become classrooms. & life becomes a love letter. It happens every day, we'd tell you. It's as simple as the moment where you add another sugar to your tea. And since the day I first met her, a Skype call that somehow grew savior-like arms-- life has been some sort of poem. And rhyming fell out from the windows and God showed up again & again &

AZURE ANTOINETTE ·

11

again. In concrete. & mimosas. & live jazz bands. & menus shared with strangers over a New York City brunch.

And I never looked back from that day.

Yes, she assured me that we were making promises to the wind that day. & we weren't going back there anymore.

Forward. Foreword.

Yes, this bound book is proof of a woman who only knows forward.

In a Matthew 10:10 fashion.

No bag. No extra shoes.

For the worker is worth his keep.

And, in case you need that message stronger. Need to hear it your ears clear. Need it as tangible and as touchable as it has been in the lives of anyone placed throughout the story of Azure's life, then you are holding the right book of poems in your hand. Her back story is intact this time.

Surely, you'll come out better than before.

—*Hannah Katy*

MOM, MINERVA & MARIA SHRIVER

» *"Do not let this universe regret you." These are the words that changed my life.*

One day in Los Angeles, I came home from work, and after two grueling hours in traffic, I flipped on the TV to keep myself company. Def Poetry Jam was on HBO, and Marty McConnell's words stopped me in my tracks.

"Do not let this universe regret you."

Naturally, this was my sign. After five years of working in human resources, I had promised myself that if I didn't succeed as a poet before the age of 25, then I would commit myself to climbing the corporate ladder. I was 24 and had just a few months left to make something of this deadline for my dreams.

So I quit. Making the decision to pursue the arts full-time was easy in this sense. A few days after Ms. McConnell's words seared my mind, I typed up a letter, as any HR professional knew how to do in her sleep, to put in my resignation. I then walked into my boss' office, dressed in my usual uniform of slacks, a collared shirt, and blazer, and when I broke the news, she didn't try to stop me from leaving. "I'm surprised you stayed as long as you did," she said.

My mind was already dancing with the possibilities of what lay beyond these pale grey, florescent-lit walls and the faux inspiration on the motivational posters that decorated them. Back in my little shoebox of an office, where a plaque showed my only real mark on the world up to that point, Human Resources Specialist, I shut the door. The hard part was calling my mother, a litigator in downtown LA, to tell her about my decision.

.../ -—-/...

I had a very structured childhood. My mom is a woman who had managed to carve out a piece of love for herself in an asphalt world that robbed her of bearing children. She adopted my sister and I in the early eighties and had a white picket fence built around the home she bought for the three of us. We were taught to study hard, clean our rooms, and we seldom watched TV, except for when she allowed us to tune into HBO on a Saturday night, National Geographic, or Maria Shriver's special correspondence.

Today, my mom doesn't remember being anything but 100 percent supportive of my career transition. But back then, I distinctly remember hearing her resistance, then dead silence, on the other end of the phone. I thought we had been disconnected by accident, so I called back, and her secretary picked up the phone. "Now's not a good time, Azure," she said sympathetically. Now that I'm a teaching artist, I understand how no parent wants to see her child struggle. Not for art, not for poems. My mom knew at the get-go what I would soon find out: The arts were a struggle. Soon enough, I was counting change in my Toyota Corolla ash tray to pay the cashier at the gasoline pump, trying to make it to an audition that I had no chance of landing. I soon had a balance of $3.34 in my checking account and had finished the last cup of Starbucks that I could afford.

After quitting, I recall descending on coffee shops with vigor, for this was my new office, and I envisioned I'd be fielding calls left and right to come and perform the one poem I had memorized, my chance to change the world and leave a mark!

Alas, there were no calls, no requests for me to perform. Just chatter, the clink of mugs, the baristas' calling of names I didn't know to come claim their caramel macchiato on their way to work. This felt like a mistake, but I was too proud to turn back. That would be receding and I don't recede.

... ll- -—»

My search began and ended with a post on Yahoo Groups for a poet who wanted to work with teens. There was no activity on the thread, given there was no pay involved, but I decided to respond. Volunteering might be just what I needed to get out of my own head. So I called, emailed, called, emailed, and left several excited voicemails that ended with "please call me!"

In hindsight, I am shocked that I received a call back, due to the fact I sounded manic with a hint of paranoia. Nevertheless, I got a call, went to an audition, and landed the role that would begin the path to my life's work.

I started as a volunteer with Get Lit Words Ignite, a teen

literacy non-profit in Los Angeles that used spoken word to spark interest in literacy. My director had the utmost faith in me, and she called me regularly to perform, to work in the schools, to change lives with poetry.

I knew each day that I was improving the lives of the next generation. I was no longer complaining without a solution. This experience was chalked full of humility, and the poetry in me was better for it. I had begun to write commissioned work that I would perform for a few different events, like the Tuskegee Airmen Col. Lee Archer, American Cancer Society's Art 4 Life Benefit, and Sundance Film Festival's eco-friendly poetry competition. I was grateful, amidst all the odd jobs I took to make ends meet and the auditions that didn't quite pan out, to be a voice for these organizations and honorable events, even if I had known nothing about them previously.

——»+++

It all paid off, because in 2010, I got the call that changed my life. My Get Lit director called me and told me that I was going to write a poem for Maria Shriver. Additionally, I was going to be flown to Sacramento to perform it at the California Museum—in just three days.

The theme that I was to write on was Minerva. Something I had very little knowledge of—enter Google, enter Wikipedia. So, with blinking cursor in tow, I read and read and read, and then I wrote.

This would be the first time that I was flown out to perform one of my poems, and when I arrived at the museum, it was nothing short of epic. There were cameras everywhere, a "green room," people calling me Ms. Antoinette, a man who needed to "mic me," and water bottles of unfamiliar brands resting on ice. I had no idea that this performance would change the trajectory of my career.

This performance felt different. After the poem ended, I was greeted by the woman I had grown up watching, sometimes sleepily listening to, in the family room with my mom and sister. The First Lady of California, Mrs. Maria Shriver.

She told the audience that she loved the poem, then holding both of my hands, the First Lady publicly invited me to recite the same poem at the Women's Conference in October. I smiled largely, tried to catch my heartbeat from racing outside the safe limits, and graciously accepted the invitation. I had no idea what her conference was about, but she could have asked me to hold a sign off the freeway and I would have smiled, just as largely, and said yes. For once, I was speechless.

Since March 2010, I have had the absolute pleasure of working with the California Arts Council on two different campaigns to raise funds for the arts in California schools, I opened the grand finale of the Minerva Awards, and I took residence in the first ever poetry issue of O, the Oprah Magazine, which Maria guest edited. One of my career highlights was being introduced by her at the California Arts Council's Million Dollar License Plate Campaign.

It was enough for Maria to say my name with a smile, but then she told the audience that every time she hears me recite, it places her "in a state of awe."

In case you haven't Googled yet, Minerva is the Roman goddess of poetry, among other gifts, and she is on the seal of California. I had passed by her every day on the flags in my school, in my corporate HR office, and never knew it. Because of her, the universe will remember me.

All I can do is thank God for His grace and for allowing me to say "yes."

//-—-//

»» LISTEN

Commissioned by Former First Lady Maria Shriver

. . . .

Listen
Take a seat; I want to tell you of
passion for compassion
Listen, if you could just lend me your
courage as I stand before you hoping
for a dose of Minervas' strength

Listen
I can't shake the memory of her, she
is 16, she sewing her way to catharsis
and healing in a detention center. In
her art program they asked her to
reflect on the qualities that comprise
a great woman, a Minerva. Then they
told her to Create, and on her quilt
she writes, "real eyes realize real
lies" where I am certain that she used
hope as thread to stitch the patches
together.
Her fabric is often mistaken as a
misdemeanor but these quilts behind
me are a chance for girls like her to

sew new seeds.

Someone asked me what does
strength courage and wisdom mean to
me collectively I said Rosalind, because
that is her name.

Listen, we are here to culminate, to
celebrate with pause—women who
have trail blazed through volcanic
terrain, barefoot amidst adversity,
hypocrisy, and the deterioration of
compassion.

Minervas have taken soot, and found
black diamonds, siphoned through
refuse and salvaged sapphires—they
have seen the beauty and harnessed
the alchemy. Minerva's are glazed
in the ceramic kiln of tumult. They
possess an authentic independence,
impeccable accessorized with warrior
strength. Yet you may not know at
first glance, she can be seen in pearls,
wearing charm bracelets, smelling of
lavender and vanilla.

Who is your Minerva, what is her
name?
Is it Eunice, Michelle, Oprah, Maria,
Sister Terry, Sandra, Helene, Lula, Ana,
Anita, Sister Jennie, Janice, Ramona,
Marilyn, Sally, Sweet Alice, Christy,
Betty, Billie Jean, Ivelise, Kathy, Jane,

Maureen, Mimi, Agnes, Gloria, Louise,
Nancy, Carolyn, Oral, or Octavia
For Rosalind, it was without question
her Mother

Yes, Minervas tell stories of truth
respect, honesty and hope.

Listen, please. Come in close, I want
to tell you that you have the power in
your lungs to bellow clear from here
to the Cayman shores when you speak
positivity. Take a deep breath, inhale
the change & Welcome to the Grand
Finale—celebrating seven years of
awareness, praising excellence, know
that it does not end here, know that it
begins again and again and again with
you...

Listen, listen to the winds of change,
smell the aura of greatness, hum a
vibration of movement and hear the
melody, it sounds like this...

--o--

Legacy is different for each person
some aspire to have their child to be
the first to graduate high school
others to carry on the family tradition
in the military
some to win the pie eating contest in
the county—what have you

OPEN LETTER TO MINERVA

Commissioned by Former First Lady Maria Shriver

....

then there are those whose path is
laid with strategic purpose of human
service
and sometimes your purpose is set
before you were just a dream turned
embryo turned almond-smelling skin
of newborn daughter

I journey on some days
yesterday I found myself standing
atop the majestic purple mountains
of California
looking out over the
ocean that glistened
with diamond fragments
Minerva seated
grizzly bear at her feet
it was all peace
mixed with determination
Minerva—meaning born from the
head
of your father—you are wisdom

And logic and intellect
Mixed with the x that your
womanhood gave you
Minerva meaning warrior
You fight for others
setting precedent for the women that
would follow her in the Golden State

If I had to speculate
I would say that Minerva is proud
it is one thing to identify that there
are issues
between the staggering numbers
of homeless, to rampant disease,
illiteracy, to, to, to
it is entirely different when a woman
rushes to the frontlines of war to save
humanity
I applaud you

the duality of purpose and happiness
is hard to understand
I am still learning many things
but on the days when I find it hard
to continue progress
I can access the stories of
"architects of change"
this world wears shades of grey so
well
and you, these women have this
amber flex about you
I thought maybe I was looking at an
aura
or the sun was resting inside of your

breastplates
or you had constellations inside of
your mouths
in dreams I saw you speak of your
work
stars fell from your lips
yes that is it
you are of the Universe in all its glory

so you should know that I have a list
of female admiration
on that list I have placed my mother,
Octavia, and Maya Angelou
 & I made room for additions
they are as follows
"sweet" Alice Harris
Betty Chin
Ramona Delgado
Jennie Hernandez Gin
Dr. Kathy Hull
Sister Jennie Lechtenberg
Janice Mirikitani
Ivelise Markovits
Captain Maureen Pennington
Christy Porter
Helen Devore Waukazoo
and
Maria Shriver

Ms. Shriver, if I may call you that
your name was etched into my spirit
by my mother at an early age
she too, recognizes remarkable legacy
and spirit in others

I remember the day was a little past
golden
we were watching the news
there you were on a screen in my
living room
she spoke of you, and your mother,
and your father and the responsibility
of public service that your family
instilled in you
she told me that it was important to
walk in my path
to stay focused
she told me of you
and from the screen I think I might
have captured your essence

yes, Minerva is pleased.
wisdom and peace never looked so
good to a tireless warrior.
I don't know if it is possible for a
goddess to rest.
I am not sure if I could send her a
message—in the event I could
I would tell her that Maria Shriver and
the Minerva recipients are carrying the
torch here on earth
and Minerva needn't trouble.
It is not about dwelling, it never has
been
for me I pray more often then not
that I will get to stay a poet for at
least another week
I was taught that you should do what
you love

Commissioned by
Former First Lady
Maria Shriver for the
California Arts Council's
Million Dollar
License Plate Campaign

. . . .

so I could stand here and talk
about per capita here and in New York
but we have enough dialogue about
that
about what isn't going right
pointing the finger is not the way this
country found independence
it is not the way that California has
continued to persevere in the ever
changing face of adversity.

so like I said
I pray sometimes twice a day
that this state will help me stay a poet
will help him stay a dancer
will continue to assist her so that she
can audition for the role of a silver
screen lifetime

you have to have faith
mustard seed size will do

trust that nothing worth having
has ever been easy
so yes to
recession, budget, layoffs
yes to heartbreak
it does no good to exist in a place
where we don't face facts

but also recall the
scent of creativity
remember that people from all over
the world
come here to get a fresh start
and it is simple in concept
we all drive
we can all afford to
upgrade an automobile plate
I will do it myself
if it will increase the budget for the
arts
we should take the breath
that it takes to complain
and hold it in our lungs
until it turns to an air of change

--o--

»» ARTS PART TWO

Commissioned by
Former First Lady
Maria Shriver for the
California Arts Council's
Million Dollar
License Plate Campaign

....

as a writer, who gives claim to God
cause he made the amber California
sunshine
it is embarrassing that this golden
state is holding up the tail ends with
Kansas on per capita spending
the stats aren't gorgeous, or even
passable
so, I'll spare you

however I am not above begging, on
my knees if I have to
cause the spending on arts is less
and the bellies of incarcerated youth
are full
and every time we close the door on
an arts program
a new wing of the jail opens

we should Create a State of
Inspiration, Independents or
Compassion
We, should have plenty of concrete
avail
so young people can architect the
foundation for change

so, I'm pleading
right along with the late Steve Jobs,
telling you from personal experience
that without art
my whereabouts in this life would be
missing
a 72-hour stint could have been 5 to 7
years
and these poems would have been
stuck in arrears
thankfully, this wasn't my fate
we had funding, back then teachers
were still allowed to stay late

simply put, the arts saved my life
right along with Frank Gehry,
Ozomatli, and Maria Shriver to name
a few
arts isn't just for those that dream in
paint
it reaches legislators, aeronautic
innovators, and Sultans
my opinion?
young people should get to try it
- ballet, even if they move with two
left feet

acrylic painting for color perspective
monologue study to increase the art
of conversation
Fairey commissioned murals and less
illegal graffiti

there's hope in that

evidentiary support proves
that minds are full of artistic vision—
not financial compromise

they say that arts is a universal
language
so I thought to paint you a picture
with words
so we'd better understand one
another
all this to say
there is little sense, throwing cents at
arts education
instead let's make this a State of
Change

MEREDITH GREY, CHRISTINA & "MY PERSON"

» *The word "obsession" has a negative connotation, so I use it sparingly. However, it is safe to say that I am obsessed with Grey's Anatomy.*

I can't get enough of the whip-smart dialogue written by Shonda Rhimes and her team, nor get over the hope that my surgeons will look like McSteamy, and I can't help but expect that all hospitals should be brightly lit and not smell like despair, urine, and Lysol. Although I'm disappointed reality doesn't quite compare to Seattle Grace Hospital, there is one piece of Grey's Anatomy I know to be true to life.

Do you remember the episode when Meredith Grey told fellow intern Christina Yang that she (Yang) was her (Grey's) person? She was "her person," the one whom she would call in the middle of the night, who's there at all times there for her. The dialogue led me to think about "my person." Who was that? Why did they deserve that title?

If you asked me today, I would tell you that I have several "people"— five at the most. At the top of that list is Sandy Glysteen.

Sandy is known to the broadcast world as a veteran producer of NBC News, where she spent 20 years in various roles on the West Coast, including on Maria Shriver's team. She most recently became Senior Producer of the Los Angeles unit of CBS This Morning. She is a graduate of Yale University. She sits on the Forbes Executive Women's Board, and previously, she was Chair of the California Commission on the Status of Women. You'd only know that if you read a press release, because Sandy is not one to tout her influence, yet she is a woman who can move the mountains of California.

You never forget the first person who puts his or her reputation on the line to endorse your work, the mover-and-shaker who gives you your big break. Sandy opened the door for me. It seemed only fitting to write her a letter. You are probably thinking that I should write her a poem. In fact, that was the one poem at which I utterly failed.

I tried to include Sandy in a poem I wrote for an event on the status of women and girls in March 2012, and she demanded that I remove her name. My respect for her far exceeds my loyalty to my work, so I gladly obliged. However, her name and essence is now in print. And the answer is no, Sandy, I will not edit this out.

.../-—-/...

Sandy,

Thank you for taking a chance on me, for mortgaging your career on my poetic call to action. For believing a live audience of 15,000 women and a million others who watched online needed to hear what I had to say. For bringing me into the same room as Oprah Winfrey and Mary J. Blige—that was surreal. Even the YouTube video that I have to remind myself to show my grandchildren someday cannot convince me that the dream opportunity you gave me truly happened.

The moments I will most remember, however, are the ones that we created in between the cracks of those momentous productions. The day that your office bought me lunch and we talked of quilts, sewn by women in detention centers, is one that I will forever cherish. Listening is a key component of my job as a writer and you make it easy. I could listen to you until the dawn.

The world's most luxurious hotel couldn't compete with the home you've opened up to me when I travel to the West Coast, filled as it is with books, awe-inspiring art, and huge tea mugs that warm the soul. I would never trade the richness of our morning conversations overlooking the canyon, the midnight Scrabble over perfectly paired wine and cheese.

You remain a constant inspiration to me, a steady calm in the turmoil of this cacophonous industry, and a majestic jewel in the crown of women I hold in high regard. I could never repay your kindness, faith, and support.

My goal is to thank you from the podium of a world symposium, from the city lines of Bangalore, India with the children of Shanti Bhavan Children's Project, from the microphone check on the evening before the inauguration of the first female president. Raising our favorite glass of chardonnay to you, I say cheers to the woman who not only taught me who Minerva was but who embodies her very essence. I take you with me, to each stage, every classroom, in all my poems.

You are "my person."

Eternal Thanks,
Ms. Antoinette (Azure)

STATUS OF WOMEN AND GIRLS

»»

Commissioned by Mount Saint Mary's College for Report on Status of Women and Girls in California

....

Reflecting on women and
perseverance always conjures visible
emotion. Reflect long enough and you
will taste the bitter, smell the sweet,
and feel the weight of bearing man,
motherhood, enterprise, and promise
in the middle of your own breast. It
isn't a wonder that some days, she
is too tired to do anything with her
hair. There must be more to life
than appearance, but let's be honest,
beauty will get you everywhere.

I bet Julia Morgan was a zealous being
to be around in her youth, bet that her
castles at the beach had moats, and
garage doors, high arches and beveled
glass windows. There was nothing that

a 17% poverty statistic could do to
derail her architect. No she had plans
to engineer a living dwelling named
Hearst Castle. The grains that rained
through her tiny palms on coastlines
knew of her brilliance, they were just
happy to be used, happy to provide
practice.

No one worried when Sally used
to daydream. She was pleasant,
docile, not bothering with earthly
physics, no she gazed—mind full of
comets, combing galaxies, meteors
for breakfast, craters for lunch, and
nebulas for after-school snacks.
Nothing about gender bias phased
her, her destiny was outlined to Ride
in a NASA fashion in a time where
man could barely walk the state of
boundary, let alone prance on the
moon.

I mean to say that, dwelling on the
low percentage of income, the lack of
female influence in places of federal,
local and state government isn't where
the power lies, it is in the lines of
Geena Davis on the silver screen, the
speeches of Nancy Pelosi, the rackets
of Venus & Serena Williams, the pen
of Alice Walker, the intellect of Hillary
Clinton, the spirit of Maria Shriver, the
heart of Tammy, Delia, Sandy, Christy,

Tracy, Hannah, and you.

Here is the caveat, you are now
equipped with the urgent information,
this will take more than four days
of American social bandwagon
dedication on Facebook profiles, and
status updates on Twitter feeds. It
will require that you get up each and
every morning, as you already do,
committed to righting the injustice,
leveling the playing field, asking the
hard questions and forgiving the past
for being unrelenting and masculine.

It does no good to be called to action
if you don't exercise your right to
move. The change lies in the "what
now." To re-empower the dream of
being a girl who plays with model
airplanes and makes new chemical
solutions in beakers, concocts the next
big movement from her high magenta
colored high chair. Give her the passion
that you had when you were her age,
show her that statistics are subject to
change, and the status of women and
girls is ever adapting. Tell her that
she is brilliant in addition to being
beautiful and majestic.

She stands at the foot of a townhome
driveway, bathing suit too small in
purple jellies, hands on her hip, and

thinks, someday I'll be able to buy all the popsicles and karate shoes I want. But today, I'll just ride my tricycle up and down the block, dream in words till mom tells me to come inside. With adopted odds against me and love folding my very existence, I now write poems for a living.

PALE PINK FILE FOLDERS & MATTHIAS

» I forget many things, more than is probably safe, but I am sure that it is only because I am moving through my life too quickly.

My mom often says that I am burning the candle at both ends, or the wicks of life are burning, or something along those lines. Her euphemisms are sometimes strange; English was a second language in the house where she grew up with her grandparents.

These days, I am starting to understand what she has been trying to say—as I desperately try to catch the big picture, I miss the small details. In the wake of the tornado I call my ambition, the memories, reminders of domestic duties, dry cleaning that has been ready for three weeks, cable bill, parking tickets, and traffic-tickets-turned-warrants fall through the cracks.

There is one detailed memory that I'll never forget, however. Around the age of nine, I felt my world shake for the first time, thanks to my older sister Delia. We got into an argument, probably about popsicles or Legos, and my quip in response to her "that's stupid" reply was, "At least I am not adopted."

.../ -—-/ ...

Quick back story: My sister had joined our family when I was a toddler. I remember going to the courthouse on the day of her hearing and our mom said that Dee could have anything she wanted. My sister, the eloquent being she was, picked a large bag of Funyuns. To this day, I still find this choice endearing. What sweetens this memory was that our mom loathed the smell of this snack, but we went to the store anyways and got her what seemed like a life-size bag. At any rate, I knew that Delia was adopted. I saw it with my own eyes and I was thrilled to gain a playmate! Now someone could help me build the gas station for my plastic orange tricycle and yellow coup in the garage.

.../ -—-/ ...

Returning to the epic argument that we were having, my sister retorted back, "Yes, you are," in answer to my "at least I am not adopted." Furthermore, she walked to the wooden roll-top desk that housed our mother's calligraphy set and monthly bills, opened a drawer, and handed me a pale pink file folder about two inches thick. This folder held legalese, official documents, and certificates, along with what I surmised to be adoption paperwork for me.

I remember sitting on the floor, reading through what I could comprehend, confused feelings washing over me. No one explained this to me. I don't remember my hearing in the courthouse, I didn't ask for life-size snacks. I don't remember. Maybe this is where the forgetting began.

.../-—-/...

For many years, I wanted to blame the adults who knew me then. Why didn't someone crouch down and tell me not to forget this, so that I wouldn't chastise my sister for her new beginning? I came from the same end. I know now that my mom just wanted to protect me. All she could say is, "You are mine, and I will love you, for everything that you will do wrong, because, you are mine. I am your mother and I will never leave you."
Many years after, I recovered from the news in the pale pink folder, and I learned to embrace it, and now I have no problem articulating this memory.

My story brought me to a place of gratefulness when a family asked me to write a poem for a fundraiser that would cover the legal fees to bring a young boy named Matthias into their home. I thought this would be a poem that taught him a little about the things to forget, but mostly, what to remember.

//-—-//

MATTHIAS

Commissioned for the Stewart Adoption Fundraiser

....

There is no biological place card

No genetic map to say whether you
Will be prone to smile first thing in the
morning
Or does your spirit fly in the evening?
We will not be certain if your legs will
be bowed like your grandfather
Is your hair more like your second
cousin or uncle (on your father's side)?

There is no nucleic code, mono or poly
To help determine why you'll sneeze
more in the summer
(Maybe it is just the climate change)
To identify who gave you your
allergies to strawberries
Nothing to trace why you are so
smitten with peanut butter (the
creamy kind)

You'll have to teach them of your
essence

They want to know you
Those predisposed dispositions are just
markers
That parents use to find reason,
excuse, comfort, and consolation
In behaviors good, bad, and
indifferent.

For those of us who are adopted...
The absence of the these markers are
irrelevant
Our identities are that of pearlized
onions,
Our families have the pleasure of
peeling the layers

They give birth to roses and butterflies
To set the world aflame with our
distinctive prowess
We are a journey sans treasure map,
no x marking the destination
And you are being sent through a
vehicle of unconventional hope
By way of your new parents'
perseverance

So your cheekbones wont match that
of your siblings
In time your smiles will be the same,
you will see

You may not like all the same things at
once,
But they love you already

It won't be easy.
There will be days where you will
question your existence
Your route to this continent
Don't spend too much time there
God has placed you in the exact place
he desired you to be
Your means of transportation is
minutia.

People who adopt are of a different
breed
They walk among Gandhis,
Faithful disciples, Mother Teresas,
angels
and "Aunt Mables" who bake pies
Just to elicit a smile for someone who
had a terrible day

Your new parents are among a breed
so small
That you almost miss them
I call them divine,
I call them lifesavers,
I call them manifestos
Because they bring definition to young
lives that had unclear lines.

They walk exalted and fight the masses
with prayer and conviction

They stroll easy among galaxies
Spread throughout the universe
because
They are not of this world.
They are focused angels.

It is true,
You won't have a map into you
Some days you will be quiet, just sit
and take it all in
You may weep
Laugh at the beckon of a new memory
You'll experience a myriad of emotions
Spanning anger bewilderment till you
reach a state
Of content.

On that day you will smile
That day you will look at your family
and
People won't know the difference,
Your cheekbones, mannerisms, family
stories
It will all echo in perfect harmony.

Don't listen to the naysayer
It is your environment not DNA
It is love not genetics that makes you

A womb only births you, the love of a
father
The smell of your mother will save
your soul
Chemical strands cannot raise you

They cannot show you how to tie your
shoes
Or spin you in teacups

They cannot buy you an ICEE
After you have been lost in the mall
for three hours
DNA can't taste iced tea with your
grandmother
(After she has spoiled you inner core
with purchases,
Chocolate and the skateboard your
mom said was too dangerous)

It is only science
It is only matter that doesn't matter
It didn't make you
And it won't love you back.

Matthias, your parents have worn the
soil here pacing
Anticipating your arrival
Your siblings are writhed in excitement
With earnest concern
I beg you hurry here.

Welcome Home.

They are all waiting to love you.

MOTOWN, LOST SERMONS & SERVICE

» *I grew up in church, starting with a little congregation in Montclair, California.*

My family had an active church life. I sang in the choir, my sister and I were youth ushers, and our mom taught Sunday school.

When there were two church services in one day, we sat through both of them. We were there all day long on Sunday. In our minds, the weekend was really only Friday night and Saturday, because Sunday was church, then dinner, then bath, then bed.

... ll--—»

Once I was old enough to make my own decisions, I stopped attending church. I had been a member of three churches by the time I was 18. At two of those churches, the pastors were asked to leave for money misappropriation, the women in the church did not depict the Christians we were taught about in Sunday school, and all three churches had "building funds," yet the needs of the actual buildings were seldom met. At this point, I suppose you could call me a skeptic and cynical of the places that took the Sundays of my childhood hostage. Once I was in college, I stopped attending.

As a young adult I found my religion in Los Angeles fads sanctioned by celebrities and Sunday brunch, which I was sure must have been holy somewhere, because all the wait staff were angelic. I decided being a kind human was more God-like than most things I had seen in church. Moreover, I rarely understood the sermons. I found them to be confusing, full of double talk. Often I felt "less" because people around me were so audibly engaged with loud exclamations of "Hallelujah" and "Amen!" I always thought, "I missed something, AGAIN." I remember seeing my mom cry in service, and always reaching over to tell her it was okay, or ask "What's wrong?" She would just pat my leg and hand me a cough drop, even though I wasn't coughing.

Giving up on church never stopped me from praying. I talked to God conversationally. I can recall saying to people when MySpace was popular that if Jesus had a MySpace, he would definitely be on my Top 8 friend list. That answer always got a laugh, I was serious though.

.../ -—-/ ...

It would be another nine years before I became a member of a church again, when Sunday once again meant 10am service and not 11am brunch. It took 28 years to hear a sermon that I understood, where my prayers went from conversation to repentance. It took God himself, a new friend, a bad church play, and a miracle to get me back in God's house on Sundays.

I had no idea what to expect when I visited New Dawn Christian Village in downtown LA for the first time, but like I have said before, I will most often say "yes" to most invitations.

The praise and worship at this new church was AMAZING! I remember thinking, if I raise my hands during a Deborah Cox song, close my eyes to a Justin Timberlake ballad, it must certainly be okay to raise my hands and close my eyes to the sounds coming from this stage. Little did I know this gospel choir that could rival Sister Act was led by professional singers, songwriters, and producers. What really shook my core was how the music was so electrifying, no boring hymnals here, yet still so well-intentioned—no clubs, no drugs, no heartbreak, just goodness and God. Secretly, I began to feel my chest tighten and recalled the vision of seeing my mom cry in church. At some point I had an "Aha!" moment, but I can't remember exactly when it was. The worship went on, for what I thought was not long enough, but it eventually ended, and now was the time I dreaded. The sermon. The time when a man stands higher than the rest, reads from the Bible, and says things to the congregation that they are clearly benefitting from, while I sat there, disconnected from the message.

For the 45 minutes to an hour that a sermon typically lasts, I would often busy my mind with poems, or grocery lists, or something else mundane. This Sunday I told myself that I would try to stay engaged. I have been told that trying, and trying continuously, is an integral part of succeeding. So, I tried and by the grace of God, I could follow this sermon from this pastor. He started his sermon with a joke! The congregation laughed and he went on to have a conversation, not preach, not instruct, just converse, integrating scripture, parody, parable, and real life. I was blown away at his instruction method. At the time, I didn't even own a Bible. I cannot recall the last time I had thought to look at the passages at all. Church had failed me so many times, but before long, I was eager for Sundays, which had never happened before. Finally, on my own volition and as an adult, I became a member of a congregation that was pastured by the man that delivered the first sermon that I understood. I should mention that the pastor I am referring to is former Motown Producer, Frank E. Wilson.

Pastor Frank Wilson has inspired me to believe in the goodness of man again, and specifically in the power of relatable sermons, and that was a gift for which I never thought to ask. He is a man of service, so it seemed only fitting to accept his request for a poem about the Deaconess Ministry that served in the congregation. His request invited me to reflect on service overall, something we could all stand to think about.

God is funny, giving you what you need as opposed to what you think you want. Real stand-up comic, that God.

//-—-//

»» SERVICE

Commissioned by
Frank E. Wilson

....

The word service defined is to obey
And to obey means that you are
law abiding, duteous, well trained,
governable, on time with God's clock
and pay little mind to your definition
of deadlines.
If I were to be transparent with you,
I would admit, although reticent,
that I often try to massage the act of
obedience to suit my situation.

Layman's terms—I forget to forget
myself.

Just in journaling my thoughts, this
poem has turned to a diatribe about
my shortcomings and I was not asked
to write a testament about my own
life—so you will have to be patient
with me.

I was asked to reflect on women, on
service, on the business of obedience

in ministry
& wouldn't you know that I had to
ask the Lord three times to help me
write this poem. I cannot seem to
draw from enough of my own life
experience to be the authority on
forsaking oneself.
So again, you will have to be patient
with me.

At first glance it seems to me that a
deaconess is a title, but stripped away
from semantics; you have a woman,
with her ear pressed to the voice of
God, where she receives instruction
on her next movement, each breath
is charted in heaven and he sends it
down at his leisure and she waits.
Living moment to moment crucified to
God's promise that He is sovereign, He
is her provider and He will never fail.

It takes a quiet strength to be a
servant, to listen to man dictate their
needs and intern fill them to the best
of your ability. You must know that it
takes all kinds, but without someone
to carry out the lethargy of tasks that
kings have found mundane, this world,
this country, this church would not
function.

Efficiency is key, time management is
crucial and the pièce de résistance is

patience.
Patience, patience to wait on further
instruction.

I have always had trouble with
peeking through life's holes to see
what lies ahead, but I am completely
taken by those who are blessed with
God's peace to sit and be still and be
quiet, with strength. This business of
serving is one that I should intern into,
and in turn, I'd turn my back away
from always having to know what
is on God's deck, cause truth is, his
magnificence would implode my mind
and I would not be able to place one
word in front of the next to write any
further, because the God that we serve
is indeed majestic.

But a deaconess is of some sort of
combination of women in the Bible,
like a concoction of Ruth, Esther, Mary,
with a hint of Deborah, infused with
God's strength. In my humble opinion
she is something like fire, something
like a miracle, something like a
walking testimony on God's grace.

We move too quick, things are so fast,
but I challenge each of you to look
around the orbit of your ego and see
just how much God has given you,
then evaluate how much praise have

you given God in return—I'll wait.

In my estimation, these women of
service to the ministry of the forward
progression of God's kingdom are
the truth. Their lives serve as a
living sacrifice and I am just so sent
by their quiet obedience that fills
amphitheaters. So we should all be
mindful to appreciate her, be gentle in
your speech and request for she works
for the king of kings and he does
not take lightly the persecution of
his people, I would hate to be on the
wrong side of that discussion. As far
as servants go, I could stand to learn
a few things, and by a few things, I
mean a host.

I will tell you this; the task of being
a servant is a direct order from God
himself.
The women that he has called into
the ministry are not your version
of convention, be careful not to
stereotype, she will run many things,
be it first lady of a congregation or
this nation, or audio visual, or human
resources, or accounting, or financial
well being, mother to a future pastor,
wife to a world evangelist, manager to
a faith-based artist—she will oversee
what the untrained eye will miss and
she will be missed if absent. He has

given us all talent and from the word
I quote: "As each has received a gift,
use it to serve one another, as good
stewards of God's varied grace."

God's word is irrefutable and our job is
simply to obey his commands.

--o--

SISTER BUNNY
& FATHERS

» *I am not impressed by what impresses most.*

As a matter of fact, if people clamor around a certain musician, create a new social media meme, or flock to the movie theatre, I am less apt to support whatever it is that holds their attention. Every now and again, however, I am thwarted by the excellence in humanity.

One Sunday after joining a new church in Los Angeles, I had the pleasure to watch a woman by the name of P. Bunny Wilson on video footage. She had taped a segment years ago on a Christian talk show and was talking about faith. In the middle of her segment, she went into a crystal clear recitation of Chapter 38 in the book of Job.

Not only was I absolutely taken aback with her ability to recall and deliver this passage, but the words that she had recited happened to be the most beautiful poem I had ever heard. The line that stuck out to me the most was when God asked Job, "Have you...shown the dawn its place." This entire passage was so powerful that I recall telling myself to close my mouth. I had never read this chapter in the Bible and I was so blown away at the fact that this woman whom I had never met committed it to memory.

P. Bunny Wilson is the first lady of the church that I joined, New Dawn Christian Village. She sat in the audience every Sunday, afflicted with a condition that the doctors coined a medical anomaly—it causes her to tremble, without ceasing, as long as she is awake.

My instinctual response when I was first introduced to her was to whisper. She looked frail and I could not get past the trembling. It caused me to tremble. So I spoke softly, which is not in my nature. I remember asking her how she was—mind you, she is flanked by two women who are constantly rubbing her hands to encourage circulation and try to bring comfort to her. The answer I expected was "good, thank you," or "fine," or something generic. But she impressed me with her response. "Grateful," she said.

Grateful was not even something that crossed my mind. I am not big on complaining. I have never seen the good in it for me. I do it, but I don't feel better for it. I thought immediately, if I were in her position, what would I have said? I am certain with every molecule of my being that "grateful" would not have been it.

... ll--—»

Some time had passed and I was invited to go and "sit" with Sister Bunny. We talked, she taught me how to work the hand massage, and after a little while I got the hang of it and relaxed. We talked about my history, love for words, my mother, growing up, and some things I've probably forgotten.

Toward the end of the day, she asked me to write a poem for Father's Day, which was quickly approaching. I definitely wanted to reply to her with a "no, I am not available" response. But Sister Bunny and Pastor Frank have this way about them that makes you want to say yes. So, "yes" is what came out of my mouth.

I went home that night, thought about her request the entire way, and just shook my head in disbelief. I didn't have anything good to say about my father. The poem I would write wouldn't celebrate dads, and no one will want to hear that on Father's Day. This time "yes" felt like a mistake.

... / -—- / ...

It was a busy season for me—I had several other events that I had been commissioned to write for, and I wrote all of those poems, cleaned my closet, donated shoes to Goodwill, found my birth certificate, and called friends I hadn't spoken to in months. The "Father" poem remained nothing more than a blank flashing cursor on the computer screen.

I didn't like fathers and had no poems for them. I didn't grow up with a father, so how could I write about something I know nothing about? Why did I say yes? What now, God, I thought, what now?

On the Saturday before Father's Day, I was pacing in my studio apartment. No poem. I remember being in conversation with God all day, my prayers went something like this:

"God, you already know, I have to perform this poem tomorrow."

"Oh yeah, and God, I don't have the poem to perform. Amen."

At some point after I had no more random acts to complete, I sat down at my desk. More often than not I write on my couch, in traffic, in bed or on the train, so sitting there to write felt almost unnatural.

I began to think about the word Father, began to reflect on the concept that God was mine. He has always been there, never left me, didn't place me up for adoption. Even then he was with me in my Hollywood studio apartment.

Sitting down at the computer, finding this answer that was always in front, on the side, and behind me, I began to type. Two pages later, the poem was written, my peace for Father's Day. I am convinced that God told Sister Bunny to ask me to write it.

I was most certainly impressed.

//-—-//

FATHER

Commissioned for Lady P. Bunny Wilson

....

Someone asked me what my Father
did for a living
I told them
my mother left the LA Sheriff's
Department to become an
Environmental Tort Attorney
they looked at me as if I heard them
incorrectly
I don't know fathers
so I default to mothers
and she is a beautiful spirit
most days
I didn't realize anyone was missing
'cause when people ask me
what my dad does for a living
my answer is: leave, he left, he never
showed up

but if I were clear
I would have told
anyone that asked me
that my daddy

hung the moon, the stars, and put the
planets in a line
so as to not disrupt the sun in its orbit
I would have told them
that he constructed an axis
then placed the earth on it
and gave it a push so that
it could spin on a slow tic
that he is the ultimate lens crafter
healer, lawyer, and most prolific poet
that words have ever seen

but that answer got
stuck in my throat
somewhere between me dancing
with my science teacher at
the father-daughter dance in the 8th
grade
and shattered promises from man who
echoed a ghost
it fell behind the phrase
"daddy's little girl"
'cause the only time I have ever been
my father's daughter is
when I played one on stage
and I didn't learn to dance
while standing on top of his feet
no, my mom taught me the waltz
so just tell people that he is not
around
I just tell people that he is not around
I just tell people that my mom raised
me by herself

but
I should have said
that my pops
built man so that man could architect
buildings
I didn't mention
that my father is God
and he gave his only son
so that we might live

so that we could love
so that we could sin and be forgiven
so that we could birth suns in sons
so that we could celebrate earthly
fathers
so that daughters could sit on daddy's
knees and
sob about kindergarten heartbreaks

To culminate
I am without an earthly father
I am a product of a mother's prayer
and God delivered me through
a different womb in 1982
when single parent adoptions
were unheard of

I know mothers
I know that I have to imagine
what it's like
to be the daughter of a Pastor
'cause I will never know for myself

but I know that my dad
I know that God
loves me from the celestial places of
the universe that we have not seen
and I am going to try Lord
to stop telling people that I
don't have one
That I don't have you.

and the next time that someone
ask me what my dad does for a living
I will just hand them the Bible
or point to the sky
or simply tell them
that he made you.

--o--

GIRLS EDUCATION, NOTES & KAYCE F. JENNINGS

» *When I was younger, I supremely wanted to attend a public school;*

they had cafeterias, lockers, huge pep rallies, arts departments and long hallways with staircases that were built for gossip and fads. Small private schools didn't have that, they had grass, outside quad areas for eating and fickle friendships, small student governments and no hallways, but the gossip lived regardless.

My mother had an alternate plan; she said that her two children were going to private school no matter the cost. If she had to go without, due to the price of tuition, then so be it. She did just that, her Evan Picone heels wore through to the pavement, but our tuition was paid, for 12 years we were in private school. Our family economics improved some time around middle school, and the balance was met, my mom was back at the half-yearly sale at Nordstroms, and my sister and I could only fantasize about the hallways and staircases of Zack Morris, 90210 and Brenda Walsh.

I say all of this to say, that I never viewed education as a gift. Education was as normal as a roof over my head. Going to school was as predictable as a sunrise, or the daily reminder from my mother to "apply" myself as I got out of the car in the drop-off lane. I credit She's the First for my now hyper passionate stance on the issue of providing education for girls. I remember feeling so enlightened when I had a moment to sit down and research the information that led my dear friend Tammy Tibbetts to start one of the leading organizations that champions for this essential cause. She's the First raises money to support girls in the developing world being the first in their family to get their education. In these developing worlds, education is a supreme privilege that most commonly is given to boys and men. A girl receiving her education is not common. Nowhere near as common as pre-arranged marriage, rape, and a life of caring for family members. I sometimes wonder how I got along for such an enormous period of time without being confronted with this issue that as of late, has seemed to steer my artistic career.

Last year, while hosting Tammy Tibbetts, super power millennial, President and Founder of She's the First, I received a call from Kayce Jennings. Kayce is the Vice President of The Documentary Group and one of the major driving forces behind

10x10. 10x10 is to the girls education movement what boom boxes and Adidas track suits are to original hip hop. Essential.

Needless to say, having Mrs. Jennings tell me that my voice was paramount to their special event for this film; that my poetry was necessary for the movement of this movement – was beautifully surprising. As I stated in an earlier chapter, I grew up watching special news correspondence, Maria Shriver and Peter Jennings from ABC News was part of the television fiber that raised me. I didn't know at the time that accepting this commission from Kayce Jennings and 10x10 was going to change my life as much as it has. But as always, I said "Yes", took some notes, and tried to prepare myself for what I knew was going to be a movement that actually made the type of noise that could be heard. The type of noise that would have interrupted the selfish teenage version of myself, which thought that education, was for everybody.

The commission was for the special event at the NYU Paley Center for the first International Day of the Girl as created by the United Nations. The event was a special introduction to the film that 10x10 was producing titled Girl Rising. Cristiane Amanpour was going to moderate the evening, a talk was to be given by Maria Arana from the Library of Congress, and I was scheduled as the closing element.

The commissioned poem was to entice the audience to join the movement that 10x10 had been tirelessly working to engineer. I was to address the film to an audience who knew nothing about the characters. The poem was to be an invitation of sorts, inviting all to listen to the voices and stories of the girls and women portrayed in this groundbreaking story told cinematically. Easy enough, or so I thought.

I remember driving home from Solvang shortly after my 30th birthday – the event was scheduled for October and I needed to come up with a poetic call to action for this cause that clearly moved the hearts of many yet needed to fall of the ears and souls of millions. I can remember feeling daunted at the task of asking people to care, to empathize with a world that didn't encourage daughters to be a stitch in the quilt of education. It angered me, so much so that the first poem I wrote was a desperate cry to anyone who would listen, to activate, get involved and help the shift that would make education a reality for girls who never fantasized about staircases and hallways that made high school look glamorous. The girls in this film, the girls that dreamt of homework and diplomas, just wanted to call a classroom home. They were dying to have the research paper assignment that I thought couldn't hold a flame to a pep rally or a winter formal dance.

I sent the first draft of the poem to Kayce, she responded quickly, her response time was always impeccable, perfectly worded and laced with the kind of grammar that said she knew journalism, that she understood urgency, and that she was about action and activation. Her response was kind, but for the first time in my career as a commissioned writer, my client, Mrs. Kayce Jennings, told me that I hadn't quite gotten it right. She told me in a follow-up email that it was "ok to be angry" about the condition of the girls education movement. She told me that the reason she wanted me to write for 10x10 and Girl Rising was because of the hope and inspiration I had given in the previous poems she had watched on YouTube. She told me that my energy was contagious, that my voice needed to be lent to the girls education movement. She told me to go back to the drawing board and try again.

I was floored, sitting in the passenger seat on the 5 freeway headed back to Los Angeles, I didn't know where to go. For the first time, I didn't nail it, it wasn't "exactly what I was looking for!", I felt like I had failed, not failed Kayce, but failed the movement, failed my profession. 2 days passed, I kept thinking about the task I was given and then it hit me. 10x10 inspired me to act, they made me feel like I used to when I was 5, that getting behind the colossal movement of girls education made me feel like I got to wear some kind of cape, like a superhero. So I wrote, about just that, the flying, the imagination of someone who is too small to ride roller coasters by themselves, but just old enough to dream big, to actually consider the possibility of the impossible.

I began to re-write, what felt like moments, fell just under an hour and I was done. Excitedly, I sent the poem, aptly titled "Superhero", off to Kayce, and took a breath. I awaited her always-prompt response. I remember the phone ringing; (I day-dreamed that she was calling, calling to tell me that she really loved it, that this time I got it right) she says, "Azure, I have a few notes". All the air went out of my shoulders and my anxiety settled near my collarbone. I didn't quite have it right, but her response was encouraging and she did tell me that I was really close. Really close was better, it was an improvement, it was something I could put in the win column, well, almost winning. The notes were easy, simple in request and I was able to execute. Kayce and I went through 3 rounds of revisions on "Superhero", each time she said, "I have a few notes". I was beginning to wonder if I would be able to get this right.

It was turning to fall in October, New York was a sea of scarves, ¾ trench coverings, jewel toned pea coats and brisk activity, which never changed, no matter the season. I made my way to The Documentary Group in the ABC building uptown and was set to meet Kayce Jennings, the client who broke my record of "nailing it on the head the first time out the gate".

That day was harrowing to say the least. For 3 hours I performed to a room of producers, show runners and on-lookers. Each time I finished, Kayce gave her "notes" and by the 8th run-through, we had all concluded that the poem was as close to done as it was going to be. The event was the next day, and there was no more time to re-write.

On the day of the show, I arrived at the Paley Center, ready for tech rehearsal, it was an eventful afternoon, I had just completed an interview with Marianne Pearl and Holly Gordon of 10x10, live on the Huffington Post online channel. The moment of truth arrived just as I was leaving make-up, the show producer told me that Kayce was ready to hear my run-through on stage. I took my place and launched into what I was hoping was going to be a decent recitation of the poem that had been poured over countless times.

During the reciting, I felt transported, I could see the very images I wrote about, almost as if I left my body to relive it some place in my imagination. I remember briefly closing my eyes, matter of fact in many of the photos my eyes weren't open at all, the poem concluded, they pulled the lights up in the theater and I set my eyes on Kayce Jennings, ready for the "notes". Even if this wasn't it, I felt honored to just be activated, to remember what it was like to have the faith of a child, the imagination that made me feel like flying was the status quo. It really didn't matter about the commission at this point. If nothing else, I was going to be a forever champion of girls education. 10x10 reached me, this girl who daydreamed of a life without private education and all things extra curricular.

Kayce, although prompt in email, observed a pregnant pause after my performance, I readied myself for the "notes", and slight disappointment from the one client who made me work to find the poem.

To quote her directly, she said, "very nice Azure, it was perfect, I have no notes.".

»» SUPERHERO

*Commissioned by
Kayce F. Jennings and 10x10
for feature documentary,*
Girl Rising

....

We come out the womb with huge
dreams, like having popsicles everyday
or eating ice cream for breakfast, being there to witness a first step, first
word, spaceships over midday skies or
feeling an entire theatre inhale a sigh
of relief when the movie ends on a
pregnant pause, we all dream of the
impact and never being too jaded to
feel it when it comes.

At some point we all donned our
parents work clothes and stomped
through the house
We folded up copy paper and pretend-
ed that we were personally steering
747's through the air – and we used
arm maneuvers that were carefully accessorized with zoom sounds to make
sure that we gave the full effect of an
speeding airplane.

We used to talk about saving the world before dinner from a fort that is made of 300 thread count sheets.

Most would agree that wanting to change the world is in our DNA.
It is centered in our imagination.
The majesty of heroes is something we all understand.
The caped crusaders, the watchmen, the emblems, colorful uniforms that almost hold a candle to Indian saris.
The power of being a part of a solution to a growing problem - conjures the kind of hope we had, when we still believed in people that could fly in the dead of night, Santa's and tooth fairies.

When you see the passion of Ruksana, Azmera, Sokha and Senna, it makes you realize that you aren't saving them; it reminds you that your contribution to their success is changing the world that we all dwell in.

Many times the joys of basic freedoms become eclipsed by the nuance of trivial consumerisms. But the sheer defiance of hope in Wadley's eyes, in Yasmin's courage, and in Suma's quiet speech let's me know that the dreams I had as a five year old astronaut slash singer slash lawyer slash veterinar-

ian who was going to save the world
as her day job is still possible. Suma's
perseverance in Nepal tells me that I
should say thank you – that I shouldn't
feel privileged for helping out, cause
in truth, I am the one being given a
gift.

The basic math is this: girls plus education equals a better world, it equals
health, safety and prosperity. When
you hear basic, you should think simple
– and simply stated, if girls are educated the nations they reside in will have
an elevated GDP. Elegantly put, the
more education she receives, the more
she will earn as an adult. She'll marry
later, have fewer and healthier children and contribute to a country with
a descending infant mortality rate.

The positives of the equation go on
and on. Basically, by educating girls,
we all get to wear the emblem, the
caped crusader garb, we get to fly in
the sky and bring the imaginations
that we have all harnessed with our
childhood memories, back to life.
That is the basic truth, the basic math.

'Cause if we threw out all of the
negative statistics, and the jargon that
makes us feel that educating girls and
saving the world isn't in fact possible,

· COMMISSIONED

72

and we just replaced it with action
and face to face communication, then
maybe for one moment it will just be
a person to person chat, you reaching
into your heart. Me, allowing myself
to travel to a land that needs no pity,
just support. And maybe, Ruksana will
show me around shanty towns with
terracotta colored clay for streets, and
she can tell me stories of her lineage
that don't include pre-arranged marriages, and sex trafficking and all the
nightmares that strip the girl of the
superhero inside of her being.

If I were to strip this equation of the
conditions of the developing world,
and just leave the faces of Suma, Mar-
iama, Lydia and Fatima, we wouldn't
have a chance to be overwhelmed
with a task that when knew we could
accomplish as toddlers, with capes and
tutu's and continental potential to do
the unthinkable.

The young women of 10x10 are like
unpredictable sunsets, sunrises and
rainbows. The joy in between the
words they don't say – assures me
that pitching in, rolling up my sleeves,
jumping in head first, saying YES to
the facts of the basic math requires
no second thoughts. Single handedly,
the stories that lie in the chests of 10

women reconfirms my desire to find
my cape again, to look at the night
sky and want to rid the world of its
indifference, makes me want to fly to
the constellations and polish the stars
because they don't shine like they
used to.

Understanding the detriment is the
first step, but realizing the potential
that lies in the mountainsides of a
world that is still developing is key.

I had forgotten that changing the
world was something I used to think
was possible.
I had forgotten that it used to be my
dream too.

»» BASIC MATH

Commissioned by
Kayce F. Jennings and 10x10

....

Basic principles of humanity that seem
to strike a chord inside the chamber
that holds the heart are always stunning, moving when we least expect it.

Somewhere in you - you are just hoping that maybe the facts have been
stretched to
accommodate the severity of the
reality.

The reality needs no garnish.
When you hear that HIV vaccinations
can change the course of a girls life
which intern changes the fate of an
entire nation you think to yourself, this
is no time to embellish.
Fact is, She is one of 77.6 million girls
that doesn't don enrollment, primary
secondary or other, she is one of the
163 million illiterate youth in the
world, she is part of the 63% that happens to be female. She lives in poverty

that seems to be the new affluent, and
if she had her shots, then she would
have the ability to know that immunizations will guard her unborn.

Yes, it would be wonderful if the basic
math were garnished, peppered and
seasoned with higher margins, larger
deficit, so that we could find some
comfort in the reality.
But the reality is the stats, and the
stats are fact, and the fact, is that
we are failing an entire gender that
doesn't know what it is like to be
considered a first world, and the first
world can't figure out how to prioritize their problems because the consumerism has handicapped our empathy.

Someone failed to mention the power
of a cupcake sale, and poems and do-
nations, cause the fact is that less than
2 cents from every dollar that is donated will actually make it to a shanty
hut, a mountainside, a favela, or slum
where there are no millionaires.

So how does one feel whole about
the arithmetic, when it is more deadly
than concentrated arsenic?

The only grace that can be extracted
from the devastation of the equations

and dismal answers is that the only direction that we can go from here is up.

This is bigger than a documentary, a moving expose or special television broadcast on Sunday evening; this is larger than a colossal symphony. She has every opportunity to beat the odds too, of pre-arranged marriages, she can eat paste and worry about sandbox arguments when she was 3, and she can learn the hard lesson of sharing her toys and not her sex. Whether it is on a golden coast or Cambodia, Egypt or India.

I have grown tired of the has been celebrities, pleading with me in the middle of a mid week situational comedy on network TV, to give 10 cents to a young girl that I know I will never meet with flies surrounding her face and dirt floors under her feet.

Personally I find the saris, the traditional garb of these 3rd worlds to be mystifying, the canary yellow and the crimson red and the cerulean blue to be bewitching. She knows her lineage – you don't need to feel sorry for her, she knows that when she goes home someday in the middle of her 5th grade year that she probably will be married off to a man that never asked

her if she wanted to still be a super
hero. And personally, I know that 10
cents a day isn't going to save her.

So there lies the dilemma, do I scrape
the inside of my artist pockets and give
her the change from the remnants
of my day, or do I roll up my sleeves,
make a push, make a film, start a
cause, champion a change, engineer
a million dollar bake sale, or write a
twenty thousand dollar poem and do-
nate the proceeds of the metaphor.

What now am I supposed to do now?

I was told that if just 10% more girls
go to school, a country's GDP increases
on average by 3%. When a girl in the
developing world receives 7 or more
years of education, she marries 4 years
later and has 2.2 fewer children. A
girl who completes basic education is
three times less likely to contract HIV.
I was also told that children born to
educated mothers are twice as likely
to survive past the age of 5 – so I am
thinking, that basically, it is on us, to
understand the soil under her feet will
ground me too, that if we just took a
break from the tragedy, and listen to
the haunting song that she sings in the
depth of the mountain cave that she
dwells in, that we can hear the melody,

that we could maybe hear a chord of
hope.

When I think of the fabric we all are
in this quilt of the human condition,
there really is no difference, I'd rather
travel to Ethiopia then, eat with my
hands, lie on my back next to her and
look up at the indigo sky observing the
constellations – and make up stories
about ancient gods using a salt shaker,
applying stars generously over the
midnight sky.

On that night, we will talk about the
simple; the arithmetic of her success
and it will never be more than basic
math.

That night, we will solve the problem.

I WILL TELL YOU THIS...

Commissioned by Alverno High School for C/O 2012 Baccalaureate Mass

....

I will tell you this…

Don't wait until you are thirty thousand feet in the air to find the beauty in the clouds.
Don't forget what it was like to be able to see 2 elephants hugging in the sky, when adults tell you that those same clouds are the sign of an impending thunderstorm. Or think that binder paper could be 747's if you fold it up right.

You are forever youth.
The sun is forgiving.
The rain brings about rainbows and if you don't have an umbrella, it's alright to let your hair get wet. He will still think you are remarkable to look at.

I will tell you this…

Today is one of many days that your
palms will sweat, retaining every
ounce of excitement fear and hope
that your family has poured into you.
This won't be the last time that you
will wait to hear your name called –
recounting what letter your last name
begins with because people are always
using alphabetical order for ceremo-
nies. It is almost as if we are all worried
that we will forget what comes after
'g' or 's' for that matter.

I have been there, sitting in the audience, hoping that an accomplishment
will finally provide my mother with
a sense on relief; I always wanted to
make her proud.

She was proud of me long before they
got to the R's for Robinson and your
family feels the same way – every extra
hour of overtime, each night spent
corralling around the kitchen table to
try and help you figure out your trig
homework and conjugate your verbs
correctly when they almost failed
Spanish themselves. It was always
about you, right after they realized
that you were coming into this world,
it became all about you.

So tell you palms to quiet down, and
just lightly pat your chest so that your

heart knows not to exit your body – the nervousness will subside and you will soon understand the success that you were destined to have. Everyone around you has always known who you are, who you will become and all the lives you will impact in the process – and they aren't nervous at all, more than likely swelling with a kind of pride that makes lions stick their chests out for the whole pack to see.

Today was eminent.

I will tell you this...

Life will start to come at you different-ly, but your saving grace is the grace of God.
Take his fundamentals with you to each trial, maintain your innocence in a world that would sooner rob you of it and never lose your identity. The world craves your authenticity; they just don't know it yet.

I can remember people with grey hair, wrinkles on their faces that said they had lived lives of purpose but had lost their way at some point. They always looked at me with constellations in their eyes when they told me I had such great potential. When my mother would send me off to grade school

she would yell out "apply yourself" as
I was getting out the car, and I think I
know I didn't appreciate it at the time.

So Today I'm reticent to say the same
adages to you, but all of it is true;
life is short,
you have a limited amount of energy
to expend don't squander what you
have been given,
no one owes you anything
and be love, as much as you can stand
it.

I have learned that there are no exor-
bitant pearls that will save you.
I have learned that reading the Bible
as an adult has reminded me that I am
forever a learning child of God.
I have learned that taking things a
day at a time is too much for me so I
choose to live moment by moment.

So, we don't have to talk about any of
it.

I still believe in fairytales, that wars
will cease.
That poems can change the hearts of
cruel men.
I am still able to sit on an airplane,
thirty thousand feet in the air, and
remember when I used to think that I
could fly.

I will tell you this last thing…

You have amazing paths ahead of you; please make small plans that are subject to change, because disappointment is too much to carry in addition to the potential in your breast. Hang onto your compassion. Continue to want better – hold the hands of an elder, pay attention to the wrinkles in their face adhere to the wisdom of dear men like Mr. Holmes – hold his lessons in your heart. Remember the feeling you had when your class won Mary's Day – cause celebrations like that only come once in your life – think about pep rally victories. I truly believe that if we had more water fights, and decorated banks the way you outfitted the teacher's lounge with streamers that the disposition of adults would severely improve.

Every now and again you meet people that change the way you see life like Ms. Tymon, Mrs. Bogan, Ms. Capra, Mrs. Fanara and Mrs. P-S and who can forget Mr. Sifter.

Life is about praying for one another, about prayer walks, Shasta's connectivity to reconciliation, its about the unabashed teenage girl love for Taylor Swift songs and quotes by Alisa Unell that spark talks. You should just focus on these memories, the life that you are to lead has already been planned, just cast your net wide, and I promise that you will catch the dream.

And if you lose motivation at some point, think of the people that have always been all about you, that wanted to be better humans so that you had someone to look up to.

Congratulations on your presence, on your arrival and know that this is just the beginning – I can tell you that.

» »

GET HER THERE

Commissioned by Girl Scouts of Orange County: Voice for Girls 2012

. . . .

When you really think about the gender equality conversation, you will find that it was never an issue just for double xx chromosomes. The issue was global from its inception, which means that it would be involving boys who revered their mothers, fathers who praised their daughters and men that adored their sisters and prayed for wives that got along with the women in their life. The need for unity on the topic is staggering, and the quicker we find a stream of conversation that mitigates the finger pointing the better we will all be for it. But somewhere between Eve, Joan of Arc and Sandra Day O'Connor, the status of women in society became an issue just for women. This is no fault of mankind, merely a bold observation that cannot be ignored.

It is not acceptable that 1 in 5 girls thinks she will be a good leader, that women only account for less than 20% of bachelors degrees in engineering and physics. As if there was only emotion, only liberating arts that stirred her psyche.

The call of empowerment is alarming - mobilizing and activating the current generation to not take computer statistics, as gospel is something that we cannot take lightly. The siren has been sounded, the daughters that you think should never grow up are chemistry majors with minors in political science, the nieces that in your mind are still missing two front teeth are the student body presidents at schools who had elected boys to run the helm for the last twenty years. We must awaken, stimulate past the feeling we know, holding fast to the ideals of change. Sometimes if you stand very still you can feel the paradigm shift.

Change is eminent, uncomfortable, awkward like a young lady whose height parallels a cathedral ceiling, with an unwieldy body, and 10 years later she is epitome of Stoic and a leading heart surgeon - she never intended to model anything but scrubs.

To name the issue solitary is near impossible, it is too vast to affix it to words that can't hold its heft. What we should remember is that the task of empowering the daughters of America means that we can assist the mothers in Tanzania, befriend the nieces in Kenya and Nepal and ultimately change the course of the statistics, as we know them.

We are closer than we have ever been before, the first female president of the United States is no longer a quest that we may not get a chance to behold, each day the same young lady who you thought wasn't strong enough to withstand a 5th grade bully, pioneers an anti bullying campaign on Youtube that goes viral in an evening, and a wallflower who never went to her prom in turn launches one of the leading non-profits to raise funds for girls education in the developing world. We are so close; you can feel a shift in the winds that is breathing an air of change. It will take all of us, embracing the condition, encouraging young girls position and helping her establish herself in a world that will only benefit from her leadership and prowess. So tell her today that she is enough, that she is exactly what we all have been waiting for. It will make all the difference, the cure for pancreatic cancer and the next social media platform will be born.

When girls succeed, so does society. Together, we can get her there.

EATING DISORDERS & WOMEN NAMED JESSICA

» *During the course of my life, I've befriended five women named Jessica.*

It was the most common female name of the 1980s and '90s, but I'd like to think the coincidence has something to do with how amazing they all are—kind, straightforward, and a pleasure to be around. My former HR manager used to form her opinions on people's character based on her previous interactions with someone who shared the same name. If your name happened to be Shawn or Derrick, you were in her good graces.

If I were to adopt this methodology, then anyone named Jessica is in luck.

The poem you're about to read starts with the third Jessica I met, in 2009. At first, it was just by phone.

... ll--—»

I drove home to the picket fence fortress to visit my mom for Christmas. The whistle of the tea kettle woke me up. Just as she had a habit of doing, my mom had started to boil the water and then was stirring somewhere outside, out of earshot to come and turn it off. I got out of bed to silence the whining pot myself, when another sound jolted me—my Blackberry rang. I didn't recognize the number, but I answered it to find it was a call from a Los Angeles-based choreographer named Jessica Starr.

Jessica referenced that we had a mutual friend in common and that she had seen my commissioned performance of "Humanity" with a group of dancers at the American Cancer Society benefit.

We spoke for a few moments about that wildly energizing evening, and then she introduced me to what would surprisingly become one of my favorite commissions to date. Jessica asked if I would be open to writing a poem about eating disorders. Not only was it a psychological issue that affected many dancers, but Jessica had witnessed a close family member struggle with an eating disorder. She wanted to send a message about the peril and pains of body image by choreographing a piece with one of her Canadian dancers.

I never thought it would be difficult to pen a poem on starvation and bulimia, given that growing up, I was just the opposite—I ate everything and anything I could find. Calories never counted and I figured I didn't fit in at school, so I might as well not fit in my uniform either.

When Jessica asked me to write this poem, I said "yes" in a heartbeat. It took me longer to process the fact that people actually wanted to compensate me to be a vessel for life's most tumultuous and vulnerable experiences.

Jessica and I talked for an hour, maybe longer. It was as if she was at my mother's table, pouring out her heart over a cup of tea, but in reality, we were just voices, trusting one another.

As Jessica told me stories, I began to revisit memories of my own childhood that I had glazed over. There was a time in middle school when my sister, 16 months older than I, would stop eating her lunch and stuffed her sandwiches under the box spring of her mattress. I remembered the night that my mom discovered them and the blank look on my sister's face when asked if she was alright. Later in high school, I could recall looking through those younger school photos, noticing how emaciated she was.

As part of the commission, I agreed to record the poem onto CD so the dancers could rehearse. I remember how nervous I felt the day I was to go into the studio. The poem I had composed in one day was all printed out on a crisp sheet of paper. But even though the ink had dried, my mind wasn't finished. I was brushing my teeth, when it hit me.

Montana, serene and quiet.

I thought of all the girls I'd never meet and how lonely I felt.

I filled my loneliness with the very sandwiches my sister had to discard under the pressure to be "perfect."

I picked up a pen, grabbed the crisp print-out on my dining room table, crossed out some lines, and scribbled in others. I knew then I had finished the poem. I was now ready to record "Look at Me."

———»+++

A few days after the recording was mastered and sent to Jess, she called me. This time when my Blackberry rang, I recognized the number. My palms were sweaty, my heart beat a little faster, and I picked up. I was certain she was not happy with her poetic investment.

Jessica had one question for me: "How did you know about Montana?," she insisted on knowing. "I never told you that we have a home there, and we visit it from time to time. Did I tell you that? I don't remember telling you that!?" It took my breath away. Once I got my voice to center from the shaking, I told her that she was correct, she never told me about Montana. I just was looking for an image of peace, and I thought about the river beds there and what I had seen in movies and books. I thought it would be a wonderful place for a quiet recovery. A place where the silence held weight.

Jessica is a good name. My old boss was right.

//-—-//

LOOK AT ME

Commissioned by Jessica Starr for MUSE Dance Company

....

bodies
they house imagination
mouths hold tongues and prophecy
collarbones give the pearls a place to
reside
your ribs hold your lungs in place
but I don't remember if I should feel
them when I hold you
I couldn't tell if you were taking a
deep breath
if I had become ultra sensitive to the
skeletal system
or if you were victim to societal
judgment

it's the latter you know
the model mayhem reality TV that isn't
reality at all
it's the check yourself out at the
grocery line check-out
laden with magazines that are
doctored perfect by Photoshop
and lemonade non-carb crazes

it's the Pepperdine mentality
the desire to not check your reflection
in reflective surfaces

you look fine

as good as you looked six seconds ago
when we passed that silver trash can,
and before that the frosted glass door,
before the polished floor,
and before, before, before, before the
after,
after, after
look at me

look
at
me

you are beautiful
it's a body
a body with curves in all the places
that aren't meant to be flat
a flesh God created
to keep your organs warm
you are PERFECT
no regurgitated dialogue, no after
thought, no measurements, no inches,
no European sizing to make you feel
smaller

what can I do to convince you?
what track can I lay across, to whom
shall I speak,

should I go to Malibu and shut down
the tanning labs, you want me sprint
to Hollywood and shut down the
stages, fire the stylist, set fire to the
paparazzi, destroy the foundation
that hides blemish, delete the dye that
camouflages roots, hostage the editors
of OK, Vogue, & Cosmo. Who has to
die, 'cause you are not an option.

you are 28, 5'10 and 87 pounds, you
think you could stand to lose a few
she is 16, a size 1 and, runs 7 miles
daily hoping to shed weight in sweat
and her, 5'6, 12, 200 pounds of
childhood obesity, binging all the way
through America's Next Top Model
marathon on E
her back seat was filled with fast
food wrappers, now she is a bulimic
alcoholic who worships Elle magazine
in her quarters at rehab for substance
abuse.
Ford Models told her that she was 3
inches too tall, so now she only wears
flats
and her skin was blotchy, hair too thin,
eyes wider than allowed, not enough
hips, she could maybe make it with
plastic enhancement

I make art, see things that others miss
I see you, wasting away, your size
0 jeans are baggy in the thighs and

knees
and I am not negligent so I won't act
as if everything is fine
the you I remember, the you I see is
beautiful
they were all beautiful, they were
good enough.

I want to help,
I want to listen but there are no words
in your mouth,
just disappointment in your eyes that
have started to set like a sodden sun.

Anorexia is the third most common
chronic illness among adolescents.
40 to 60% of high school girls diet.
50% of girls between the ages of 13
and 15 believe they are overweight.
80% of 13 year old girls have dieted.
40% of 9 year old girls are dieting
now.
that that 20% of people with anorexia
who do not get treatment will die.
About 80% of those who do get
treatment don't get enough of it;

but there were no names, no faces,
no relation, just text, they don't know
that "that girl" is somebody's little
sister, daughter, girlfriend, Godsend,
best friend, they, those statistics, didn't
know that it was you

it makes me nauseous to hold you and
feel the ridges of your spine
I am filled with regret to know that
your organs are cold due to the
absence of your flesh.
but I'll hold you, TIGHT
I promise
you know we could go away, to
Montana
where the only reflective surface is the
fly fishing riverbeds
and I will board up the mirrors in the
cabin as to not disturb your peace
yeah, we could have breakfast
the kind of pancakes that are dressed
in maple syrup
that kind that they make in New
Hampshire
and you only have to take a bite
and you will keep it down
and I'll keep it down so you can get
your rest

I want to help you
I want to listen
but there are fingers in your mouth
where there should be words

Look at me—you're beautiful

Look at me

--o--

>> >> # GET UP

Commissioned by Jessica Starr for MUSE Dance Company

....

I can't be honest and tell that I know
how to take a deep, long, breath
unless it has to do with me being
stressed
there's no app for it
the getting out of bed
or hiking for clarity
or stretching for patience
you gotta go to yoga for that

there's no digital add-on
that can replace a run at sunrise

I have looked
high and low
and the search results have yielded
none
it wasn't that long ago

I can remember
jungle gyms

childish laughter
screams of excitement
because recess had finally arrived
but adulthood soon followed
recessive climates clicked on the heels
of a loud
active millennium
but amidst all that
I can still hear nature
physical health is crying like a siren in
background amongst the stars
just begging us to come out and play

it's like a converge
moving toward a destiny of
activity
movement has no intention of going
quietly
it's saying

get off the couch
away from the sectional
you will step
depart from the rectangle box
adorning
your wall
broadcasting false realities

this is only about the outside
the boundary of the deep
the rolling
right in it
down the hillside
laughing until pain accessorizes your side

this is about movement
this is about living
moving
oozing limbs

to a beat
let's just take a moment
take a long
deep
breath
recall the sunshine
your dreams of brooks babbling
kindergarten stretch
siesta and morning jogs that have now
turned into chaotic sprints
to work
imagine, you aren't late
that movement is peace
and your body is pleased
to inhale the serenity
exhale the toxins
embracing the doctrine
of living
one day
at a time

or savoring the quiet
while the chaos sleeps
this body
these bodies are temples
crying for the sunset
yelling for the fresh air
begging for less air conditioned
environments

and more natural habitats
it's saying to you

get up
get up
no smoothie
no Starbucks networking
just you and me
no app, no rules
just living
all the bodies just quaking to the pulse
that is activity

get up

elevate your resting heart rate
and get up

it's begging you
it's begging me

to get up

»»DIVINE DIRECTION

*Commissioned by
Jessica Starr for
MUSE Dance Company
Show "Divine Direction"*

....

Have you ever seen 2 filmmakers
entranced by thunder and taken by
lightning from 30 thousand feet in
the air? I have, it looks like 2 adults
that haven't had the chance to be
friends anymore, the kind of friends
that you make when the sand is in a
box, parked in the middle of a gravel
wasteland that the adults call a play-
ground. Like life steered them through
the carpool lane and they didn't get a
chance to edit and play hide and seek
with the rest of the class.

But we shared a row, the movie buff
near the window, the photog in the
middle, and me, the poet in the aisle.
Three heads starring out of a window
far too small to house our imaginations. Together we watched the celestial magic show, in a transfixed state,

as the lightning moon-walked across the sky scape for seconds at a time, until the thunder grew tired of taking second place. At one point, the thunder took in a deep breath and made the entire sky shake like the decade of the 1980's – it was like having bass in the galaxy. The crash of the elements was enough to put me in my place, if my place were the younger me, 4 years tiny, full of intrigue, yet terrified that the clouds and the stars were screaming at one another.

But to these two, this celestial clamor wasn't to be regarded as danger, even hanging mid air in a steel bird with grandparents and newborns on board. The way they marveled made me think that to them, this electric, timpani and cymbal event in the sky was like witnessing the children of Greek gods sparring with each other, striking matches on the floor of the sky, thus rendering white, hot flashes in a purple spread. Never mind, the massive 747 hanging 10 in the mass of the night sky. Watching them, watching it, was like viewing the epitome of fearless. It was like terror was their muse, like they just danced with danger and possibility.

At some point, I thought, maybe this is
right.
Maybe this is how it all ends.
We all descend in a glorious blaze of
thunder, accessorized with lightning
for bling.
Maybe the gods will spare us the pain
of landing in an earth that would
rather see you broken and not knowing your worth, no muse, not inspired,
no fire in your belly.
And with the all this turbulence about
us, maybe I should have been listening
to the instructions that the flight attendant gave those us of seated in the
emergency exit row.

But maybe, I will just enjoy the show
with these people who make movies
and take pics and make choreography
beg for a drink of water.
Maybe, the definition of thunder is
really a black star laughing and maybe
all this white light is a new nebula is
being born. Maybe the sky was always
a pretty eggplant purple, something
robust, far louder than the sound of a
failing airplane engine. Maybe, we just
trust, and don't put up a fight going
down, maybe we just dance until the
music in our head stops.

I should just stare out into the black

AZURE ANTOINETTE ·

105

space like those humans I shared a row
with.
I should just FLY.
Wings open with cinema on my mind,
sparks in my fingertips, prayers on my
lips and silver screens flashing before
my eyes. Yea flight attendant, just
open the doors, let the oxygen masks
drop, no seat belts, slide through the
galaxies, eyes wide open, keeping my
pupils peeled, for little Greek gods,
striking matches on the floor of the
sky.

Maybe, I just say yes.
Maybe, I should let the chaos be my
muse.
Maybe, I just take it as divine interven-
tion.
Maybe, this trajectory, all this lighting
and thunder is merely Divine Direction.

»» RED MARKS

Commissioned by
Jessica Starr for
MUSE Dance Company
Show "Divine Direction"

....

the red marks on the bathroom wall
are the way that i keep track
of each day that you say nothing

most days, you stare into concave
spaces
rather than connect with my face
the space that you told me felt like the
home your mother never made for you

babe, I miss your eyes

i haven't seen them hazel and honest
since our 7th date
in that town square that was still akin
to 60's style promenades
remember that you walked me near
the fountain
brushed my hair behind my ear
choked back the urge to tell me

that you were falling in love
and instead asked me
if i had ever had my heartbroken

i told you
yes

the only truth i could stand to utter at
the moment
i told you that my heart was a mere
fraction of what it used to be
i told you that one of the galactic
quadrants was insanely decorated and
smattered with my coronary matter
matter of fact, the destruction was so
extensive that i have trouble being
held, that I don't like it when somebody inhales me in
that i never think my love is enough
that my love resembles a mangled
chain link fence that has been worn
down by derelicts and recession
i told you that i am massively insecure
that i believe that fairytales are for
girls that don't look like me

then i remember pausing
looking at the crows feet that perched
on the side of your then honest eyes
and asked you
"will any of this be a problem?"
with all the care you could find from
women who were born to bear great
men, you told me no

you told me that it was fine, you
brushed my fly away hair behind my
ear and told me that I was beautiful
gorgeous even, so much so that you
couldn't stand to focus on anyone or
anything else. You told me that you
would tell me everyday
you said that you would take up space
travel so that you could find the pieces
of my heart that I left unattended
you told me all of that

You lied.

i just mark the wall with red lipstick
for every single day
that you don't say anything

MOTHER'S APOLOGY

Commissioned by
Jessica Starr for
MUSE Dance Company
Show "Divine Direction"

....

I was trying to find the words
Trying to articulate my apology
It could be easy
Easy as me saying that I am sorry
That seems insufficient
But you don't understand
I thought it was just that one time
Thought that I could grab some cover up
And cover up this blue-ish colored
flesh around my eye
He was just a little baby, moon walking
in his socks
Stalking the Michael Jackson videos on
TV
He was too little to protect me
You should have seen him as a young
man
My baby boy Chris was striking
And yes, he used to see him strike me

I'm really sorry

It's no excuse
When he would cry
I would use it as an excuse
To cry too, and he assumed I felt his pain
He was little, I let him believe that I was
Just devastated that he scraped his knee
It was more than likely
A shattered rib, busted lip
Bruised pride, that brought me to tears

You know
We used to hold each other, tight
In the quiet mornings
I tried to impart maternal words of
wisdom to him

I always told him
Christopher Brown,
You never put your hands on a lady
But in the middle of his break dance
practice
Or when he was practicing his freeze
frame
He used to say
Mom, I want to be a grown man
I want to do like adults do
Have big kid drinks
And make sure that people know my
force

So naturally, he modeled his daddy
And baby girl,
I am really sorry
That my Chris put his hands on you

111

»» MISPLACED

Commissioned by
Jessica Starr for
MUSE Dance Company
Show "Divine Direction"

. . . .

Adam Lanza.
I have sinned, many times over, many
times too many to enumerate.
So if hell is real, (and I truly believe
that it is) if hell is where sinners go,
then I will do my best to just keep my
judgments to myself when I pass you
in the hallways adorned with fires that
would make the charred hillsides of
Malibu nervous.

But Adam, where was your journal, it
must have gotten misplaced with the
sections of a childhood that teach you
to forgive your enemies for not letting
you get on the swing that you waited
patiently for at least 84 recesses.

Adam where did you loose your prose,
who stole the stanzas from you that

held the kind of promise that is only reserved for toddlers.

Explain to me how you went son, who never really communicated correctly turned gunman saw it fitting 11 days before Christmas to take the lives of 20 children who were tasked with just remembering bring home the right jacket. The one that her mom wrote her middle name in. She didn't want her baby to get confused (there were too many little girls named Ashley). They must not have understood whom you were when you came in the class-room with guns blazing, they must have thought they were in a movie, and then the bangs began. Then the blood began to fill the very mats that they took naps on.

Adam, why take the aggression of an AK47 into the learning space of young presidents, botanists and princesses pumping their boogie monster scared cavities full of the very bullets that were assailed at your carcass clearly rcvd. You should have been a scien-tist. You should have been the sharp shooter that we sent to the front lines on the morning of September 12, 2001 as to rid the world of the terrorists.

What did you do with your haiku?

Adam, as I continue sinning, as we
both continue to be living me in the
present and you in the memory of
sister who had to lay her older sister
to rest cause she only wanted to be a
principal; I pray that I find some sort
of prose to explain to the mothers of
babies that were still little in the eyes
of the world, why they had to bury
their hopes 11 days before the birth of
Christ.

Adam, this cannot ever happen again.
We have to control the impulse to
move our trigger fingers off the pistols
that have the power to end promise.

»» CONFIDENT

Commissioned by
Jessica Starr for
MUSE Dance Company
Show "Divine Direction"

. . . .

I'll take him home with me tonight
And I don't think it tawdry
I see it as knowing what I am capable
of
I see it as power

I have always known that behind these
Breasts is a heart that may not know
how
To love you honestly
So up until tonight
The tone was off key, and the whole of
the beats sounded lonely

And as much I am protest to under-
stand much of nothing
I do know the anatomy of my body
I know that I have two hips
One that one day will rest the body of
my toddler son

One that will give me more arthritic
trouble when the weather is poor
But tonight, these two hips will twitch
side to side
Echoing the way waves dances in a
tsunami
I have a mouth that in the day light
Will never say enough to make you
pay any mind
But these lips will steal your attention
when they
Slide down the side of your nape
I understand my body
And I don't call that tawdry
I call it seduction
I call it hurricane
I call my aura monsoon
I call this level of my persona
A category 7
Something there isn't a name for

But I will call your name
In a way that mother never said it
Tongue and cheek
Rosy
Fast paced / Bated breaths / NC-17 /
never rated G / Just me
No apologies
Ever aware
Of exactly
Who
I
Am
And

Some call me harlot
Some call me poison ivy
But some call me miracle

Him, he doesn't know what to make of
me
And it's fine
I will walk by him slow
Let him breathe me in
And then
I'm gonna take him home with me
tonight

IN RE: TO BAD RELIGION

»»

Commissioned by
Jessica Starr for
MUSE Dance Company
Show "Divine Direction"

....

they said if you don't speak it has no
life
so i would love to look back and see
our past still glistening like new things
do
but when i even peer over my shoulder
that only understands muscles and
atrophy
i see ruin
i see thunderstorms and a perfect
recipe for disaster
i don't get to recall the way your name
tasted in this mouth
that was always the envy of the eyes
that got to look at your aura

i cant do both
look at you
and watch my mouth

· COMMISSIONED

118

there must be some cadre of humans
that understand the chasm
of where my heart used to reverberate
at the thought of your arrival
in my periphery
memories these days are as expensive
as forgiveness for a family that would
rather see us broken then deal with
the reality of our bliss

PEACE AND BBOY TALK

Commissioned by
Jessica Starr for
MUSE Dance Company
Show "Divine Direction"

....

Kickstands
Freezes
Poses
Blow-up
Stand up straight they tell me
They tell me to center my mind
They tell me to try yoga
No soda
Just focus
Let the sunrise be enough for you
But there aren't enough minutes in an
hour
And there are too few seconds in a
minute
And in the moment is some place that
I have trouble living

Oh for peace
Oh for peace sake
Oh for the sake of chaos

I should get acquainted with the mis-
ery
So when the joy pokes it's inflated
through the mundane
Then the sunshine will be sufficient
Ride my bike
Chase the sunset
Get off slow
Freeze my frame
Pose along the horizon
And extend my kickstand
Ode to peace

HEARST, TWITTER & TOAST

» *Seems like yesterday, I was driving in my black Honda Accord named Carmen, turning left onto the street I grew up on, and the phone rang.*

Albeit against the law, I answered it, and the person on the other end of the line caused me to hit the curb and speedily drive off, as to not be seen at the scene of the crime. (No one was hurt, just my fender and the curb.)

The other voice was one of the chief editors at O, the Oprah Magazine, calling to see if I had any interest in being interviewed for the first-ever Poetry Issue, guest edited by Maria Shriver. This was shortly after the Minerva Awards in 2010. I was now in talks with three lecture agencies that were interested in signing me to their roster and newly out of the volunteer job that I had thought I would never leave. Overwhelmed is the only word that comes to mind. While listening to her, I very distinctly remember thinking, "My life is getting ready to change drastically, again." I told myself to calm down, to not be outwardly excited, because someone poised would take a moment to think this over, someone seasoned would have a grounded tone, someone with artistic experience would maybe take a meeting. But let's be transparent, I was not poised; I had on basketball shorts and a hoodie. I was not seasoned; I was salty, sometimes overly peppered, with realism. I was no artistic veteran; I was a zygote, an embryonic thought in the mind of the artistic scheme. So, as calmly seasoned, poised, and veteran-like as I could, I replied, "Interested? Who would tell Oprah they were not interested! I am more than interested! YES!" She laughed, we talked candidly, and my palms slid off the steering wheel just as I parked my car in front of the white picket fence fortress, which now that I am older, just looks like my childhood home.

I walked in the house, greeted my mother with a kiss, and said, "Hey mom, I am going to be in O Magazine."

... ll- -—»

I watched the calendar closely as the magazine's newsstand date approached in March 2010, wondered about how my interview would translate to the glossy pages, and daydreamed about the domino effect that could happen. Everyone knows, once Oprah says you are okay, you're set. With the "O" golden validation, I could fill up my gas tank and not worry about checking my account balance.

March was here, the April Poetry Issue came out, and it felt surreal. There my name sat, along Nikki Giovanni and Robert Frost. I was on the same pages that contained quotes from Maya Angelou and Pulitzer-Prize winners and poet laureates. Unbeknownst to me, more content from my interview was posted at Oprah.com. I was grateful beyond words.

Riding high on a cloud far greater than the exponent of nine, I was trolling the Twitterverse on my Blackberry phone. I ran a search for keywords like "poets," "National Poetry Month," and "New York City." A RT (that's re-tweet, or reposting of a 140-character message sent by another, for those who don't speak social media) returned from an organization named Girls Write Now. The tweet said that She's the First, another non-profit, was looking to partner with a female poet for a National Poetry Month workshop in Brooklyn. I replied, and when She's the First tweeted me back, we followed each other and exchanged email addresses via private direct messages. I sent my one page from O Magazine, biography, and sheer interest in being their poet of choice, which landed in the inbox of the founder of She's the First, Tammy Tibbetts. That evening, she and I started a dialogue on the phone, and I began to feel the same as I had in my Honda the day O Magazine called. Life was changing, again.

She's the First is a nonprofit that raises funds for girls' education in the developing world. They had just teamed up with the Young Women's Leadership Network, all-girls schools in the New York public school system that focus on providing college-bound education for young women. The Young Women's Leadership Schools of Brooklyn, East Harlem, Astoria, and Jamaica have access to private funds that provide programs that the state cannot afford to bring to the students.

Tammy told me that She's the First had no money to pay me, but they would love to have me. She mentioned that by day, she was the social media voice of Seventeen, located in the Hearst Tower in Manhattan, the same building that was home to O Magazine. Her roommate was even an editor at O! The connection was so strong, and my world was getting smaller. I told her, "Yes, I would be honored." I cashed in my frequent flyer mile tickets on Virgin America, paid the $2.50 balance, and I was off to Brooklyn.

I arrived early morning from a red-eye flight. I arrived at the Young Women's Leadership School of Brooklyn, beyond eager, not knowing what to expect. But it didn't matter. I was in my favorite city in the world, it was National Poetry Month, and I got to work with teenagers and recite my poems. Everything was right.

The heads of educational programming from the Young Women's Leadership Network corporate office had come to observe the poetry workshop. I shook their hands and got to work.

An hour and a half later, it was over. The day was a smashing success, the class I spoke to was lively, honest, and endearing. Tammy and I hugged as if we had known each other since grade school, and the ladies from the educational programming department invited me out for toast. I was going on and on about bread that morning. Luckily, they found it funny, and one of the women even shared my love for the simple breakfast treat. I said, "yes," and we strolled to a café in Williamsburg.

They told me about this network-wide summer camp

that they had, involving schools in three boroughs. Together we conceptualized how to stretch the one-day workshop they had just observed into three weeks, how to bring creativity, voice, and writing to a program that was missing an artistic vision. They offered me a new commission: Poet-in-Residence.

We'd go on to publish an anthology of work titled "You Should Know This About Me." This was a free write prompt that I had created to get young people to talk about themselves, to break the ice.

I was going to be in New York for July of 2010.

Life changing. Again.

Saying "yes," again.

One tweet. My life changed in 140 characters or less.

//-—-//

»» AFTER.WORD

Commissioned by Young Women's Leadership Network

....

Cannot count the amount of times I
have had writer's block.
but I desperately want to write you
a poem that you can be proud of—
something you can read when we
don't see each other anymore, and
think—this was heartfelt, she wrote
this to me. But I want to tell you, I am
scared.

When I was 11 or 12 or 13—I know I
never had your courage/stayed quiet
about the things I was going through,
and if I had a younger me to spit
wisdom to, I would have told her to
befriend young women, like you, and
you, and YOU.
remembering some days hurt, or are
just difficult altogether, but in a dream
somewhere when I was still cradled
by innocence, I thought I may be an
inspiration—that is, if I can stand to

127

make it through all of this. who knew,
it would be you who inspired me.
AWE.
only word I can conjure out of this
jaded lexicon.
Know—YOU INSPIRE ME.

And if I were honest, which these
days is painful too, I would be forced
to tell you that I am deathly afraid of
not leaving a mark—'cause you have
made an impact on me by just being
yourselves, telling your truths, and
reminding me the glory of dodge ball
amidst your home lives of molestation,
broken family, and adult-told half-
truths.
I applaud you—young women.

So I guess this is some sort of open
letter or dear Jane, to say thank you
from the most earnest place I can
access for your willingness to take me
in and settle into a poem each day.
Communication is a dying art, when
you are older, you will understand.
You should know that I think you are
modern day superheroes, and I won't
explain that to anyone who can't see
what I see.

When I read your thoughts, my heart
beats in time with nautical knots and
I thought, was that the sound of a

10 car pileup or am I still able to be reached? Continue, young women, this world needs your brilliance, and again, thank you for inviting me in and letting me stay a while.

--o--

KICKS, PELVIC REGIONS & BEATS

» *I love tennis shoes, kicks, sneakers—call them what you want, Nike is to me what Louboutins are to Carrie Bradshaw.*

All I have to do is watch a Nike commercial and I am already sold, telling myself, "Azure, you need a new pair of kicks, now." If only I had been commissioned to write about footwear! While that hasn't happened (yet), Nike did appear in my poetic life when I was least expecting it—and no, not on the soles of my feet.

————»+++

In August 2011, a man named Omar Johnson sent an email via my website and identified himself as a marketing executive that worked for Beats By Dr. Dre, and they (Beats) thought I would be the perfect writer for a new campaign idea. Now, hats off to Google, I immediately verified that this was NOT spam, and using my CIA techniques, I found that Omar was a former marketing VP at Nike. This looked promising. "I don't know what they want exactly," I remember thinking, "but maybe they will give me some free shoes. I would write a poem for shoes!" Then I began searching Beats by Dr. Dre. I had heard about this epically priced, non-recession-friendly headphones company, but I did not know much else about it. The website was understated but popped in all the right places. My research led me to conclude that Beats was an empire with mogul status. And was I ever right.

After some email slash phone slash voicemail tag, Omar and I were set to meet. Instantly, I knew that this was a change of pace for me. For a while, I had been on the women/girl empowerment circuit, and nothing about helping a corporation make money was emotionally uplifting at first. When I arrived at headquarters, which was designed for sound, just like the headphones are, I found all the furniture in the lobby to be white. Omar's office was set off by plexiglass, not solid walls, and the floor was littered with headphones, speakers, and Nike shoe boxes. It was pretty much my dream home.

The commission talk began as I stood alongside Omar at a shoot for the promotional photographs for the Million Dollar Headphones, which are encrusted with real diamonds. You may have seen them on LMAFO at the 2012 Superbowl. The fact that there were diamonds in headphones, that the model posing with them was topless, and that the retail price was one million dollars is something that we will not discuss. But I have set the scene for you. I sometimes have to pinch myself, to believe that this is my life, this is actually happening.

Later that day, Omar came over to the table I was writing at, and he said one of the most unforgettable phrases to me. "Azure, I want you to talk about how Beats headphones make you feel," he said. "Like when you put these on, what you are going through, we want to say that you feel the sound in your crotch hair." Crotch hair? Stop, wait, what?! I am now the owner of five pairs of these headphones (not the million dollar variety), have listened to several genres of music at skyscraper volume levels, and never has the sound affected this region of my body. I had to laugh. What was awesome about this VP was that he was dead serious. He wanted to create a campaign about the visceral activity that these headphones produced. This sound wasn't for the audiophile. This was to re-inspire a love of music, to initially bring about the feeling of a melody that I can definitely remember from mix tapes. This was to inform the current generation about the beauty of music made in the studio, the feeling the producers had when they mastered a track, and the essence of sound before iTunes compressed it to a generic level that lacked feeling. He thought a hair-raising reaction, granted in a pelvic region, set the bar.

I accepted the challenge. This project by Beats is coined "The Manifesto Project." The challenge to raise hair, to invite goose bumps over a love for something as universal as sound, is something I was honored to do.

Like I said, I love shoes, but before kicks, I loved the beat. Stillviscously love the beat.

. . . .

These kids spend their parents'
Benjamins
on devices to hold 80 thousand songs
but stuff plastic pods in their drums
and hum along
I say silence your opinions, put your
voices on mute
I say you don't know nothing about
the truth of a melody
You don't know about how the last
verse of a manifesto
Could make you want to point the end
of a berretta at some wannabe
Who always thought he was gangster

This is to you
First off, skinny jeans don't pack heat
and knots like the way sags used to
This is for you
'Cause you ain't never had to do
surgery on the top of a cassette tape
That held the only reason it made it
okay to ride two buses and three trains
to a school that didn't know nothing
about superman coming to save them
Your generation ain't never felt a hook

slide into their chest and make their
heartbeat beg for mercy
Ain't never heard an intro give a
grown man Monarchs in his stomach,
taking wings—'cause he didn't ever
think he could love another woman
again after a stray bullet claimed the
life of his baby sister
You ain't never heard a bridge that
made you want to jump off the one in
Brooklyn and make it,
Till now.
Till this beat.

--o--

....

I never forget the day that I had my
first audio crush
He was a man with a method and she
only had the 411 on what she'd been
through
And I ain't never heard somebody call
me baby other than my momma
But I believed both of 'em when they
crooned that I was all they needed to
get by
My heart was torn out when they
sampled Motown into hip hop
Left adorning the grate of speaker on
a Magnavox boom box
I kept looking for the sex of it
In the middle of the hole where the
ear goes
Or where my head slides in, adjustable
for width
No one told me—That I would find the
Bass line on the inside of my
metatarsal
Or that my ACL would soon pop going
down the steps trying to catch the 6
train

'Cause it's been a minute since a song made
Me want to shake before the crump was out
But I couldn't find the grind that
Marvin Gaye
Sang ballads about
At best
I fell in love with Friday night deejays,
or New Year's Eve playlist
That would sometimes do the trick
And play body instruments
Felt like the sound was sourcing
Blood entering inter-cross sections that
bring about creation
Sensations, trembling, and now this seems
inappropriate
Blood coursing through my veins
Headed straight for collision
And all this 'cause the song just started

It's a good thing they didn't make
headphones like this
When Biggie and Pac was out
'Cause when you young you lack decorum
And you don't know God yet
You ain't never experienced
disappointment outside of a frown
from an elder
But when heartbreak, lies, and deceit
round your sphere
Music is the hole you draw near

And your prayers have vibrato
And you go to a booth just to let go.
I could imagine
The virgin I'd never have been
'Cause the sound entering drums
Certainly would have popped hymens
And high mans run around these cities
bobbing and weaving
Desperately seeking to translate sound
into visceral feeling
And I think Dre's onto something
My hair follicles are at attention and
all I'm doing is listening to a Beat.

--o--

»» #4

....

I'm no audiophile
Not a hi-repro sound junkie
Give me life, give me live, I have little
to no need to reproduce that at home
I'd rather hear it for the first time,
every time, on repeat

Not hanging out reminiscing
About vinyl circles sending baby
boomers into fits
Got little interest in the amplified
glory of line levels, semiconductors,
valve technology or high impedance

Gimme a Kanye shrug and a sample of
Otis Redding,
and make sure I can hear the gum pop
of the audio technician on the outro
so I can feel like I was in the studio
when the producers were magic in a
pro tools caldron

You gotta understand
I grew up on Maxwell brand blank
tapes
Taped overtop mom's gospel joints

Just so I could catch the jams on
Saturday morning

I fell in love with hip hop right after
my momma
Told me about God

And now I'm thinking
Pink was kind of onto something
Cause deejays were definitely heaven
sent
And I'd rather go to that church
the one with the beats

--o--

» » #5

....

I remember when I used to club with E
Used to grind on speakers
'Cause I'd just love the way bass kissed
my hips
And snares always used to crawl up on
my collarbones to tell me secrets

Never did I think I'd get the same
sensation inside my ear drum
In a place that didn't reek of two-day-
old Hennessey
Tramp stamps, magnum wrappers,
and the dreams of father's who never
wanted their daughter's nickname to
be "Misty, Stormy, or Honey" to men
that never knew her when she was little.

I was walking east on Lafayette
Crossing Bleecker
And there it was
The climactic introduction
To that "secret" bass line

In 10th grade bio
they told me about the sensation of a
goose bump
that the chemical makeup was

similar to endorphins
but I know endorphins
feels like heartbreak downed with a
shot of wind sock
cold chill, slap in the face, I'm cheating
on your with your best friend, and she
isn't your mother.
I know endorphins, I seen chemicals,
I used to watch her snort 'em, Shoot
'em, walk away, tell me its gon' be okay
No, I know what that looks like.
No, this was hair raising,
Twitter trending
This was anatomic implosions
Galaxies falling out of my canals
For a moment I just turned up the
volume
Bent back the spoon, held it over a
flame, inhaled the scent of burnt half
notes
and swooned in bass
I didn't know I'd ever hear a playlist
sound like guttural screams

I remember when I used to club with E
Used to just turn my back and grind on
the speakers
'Cause I'd just love the way bass kissed
my hips
And snares always used to crawl up my
spine
perch atop my collarbones to tell me
secrets about the beat

--o--

....

Daydreaming is dangerous
I wanted to be a knob on the sound
board
So you could turn me left until we got
it right
Where your index and forefinger
gripped me to send me south until
The pitch bended enough for me to
squirm
This was me wanting to be in more
than one place at a time
So that my body looked like a post
9/11 skyline
This was fictional, this was galactic
This was maternal
There is something about this beat
that makes my pelvis sing
Something about it, that makes you
sexier than you have ever been
Something about this hook that makes
me think that you could be the one in
the candlelight
I could never claim you in the daytime
Something about this lick has me
transfixed
Blending into choruses that will not

worry about forgiving me in the
morning
Verses that have no problem leaving
money on the nightstand
Bridges that loved me only long
enough for a one-night stand
This feeling was ecstatic and sees me
running to Duane Reade for Plan B the
next morning
Heads sliding under bass bridges
Wishing I could just stay here
Where I can barely hear my inner
thoughts
Take me back, I'd rather sit Indian style
on your lap/I mean your sound board
Whoring myself through for another
outro
I rather cross my legs across your snare
than hear one more melody the way it
wasn't intended
I'd rather you sit in between (the
monotony of traffic and lies)
Send me, you send me.
Press Play

--o--

JADE, TAKING TURNS & THE WORD NO

» *There are days when the tenacity of the teenage generation overwhelms me.*

"No" isn't an option, garages are homes to music labels, and a dorm room can become the initial headquarters to the world's largest social media platform. They obviously are very familiar with the word "yes" as well. This generation doesn't worry that their creative genius won't catch fire. They know with a moral certainty that it will. And when it does, the product of this genius will go viral, like an electronic inferno.

When I was a senior in high school, my daily thoughts were about superficial damage control, quad festivities at lunch, what the senior class prank would be, and how we were going to stun the audience with our silly string pies de resistance during graduation.

Bullying was not yet prevalent, cutting was not fashionable, and eating disorders were still private family affairs. There were no Kardashians, the Real World on MTV was the only peek we had into what happens "when people stopped being polite and start getting real" as adults, and the creators of YouTube were probably at fifth grade recess. We passed notes, not text messages; we hung out in the quad eating breadsticks after school; we paged each other; we talked on the phone using caller ID to check if someone was worth switching conversations for—there was no texting while chatting while Skyping. Things were simple.

But there also was no cry to change the world, no Kony, no Million Hoodie marches, no profile angst and status updates. If there was a problem happening in the world, we discussed it in classes that were debate-friendly and left it in the room once the bell rang for dismissal. Hosting conferences on how to change the world was for adults. We were kids. We worried about dances and 'N Sync and nacho cheese and Dr. Pepper. There was no torch we had to carry, just our books in cute bags.

Today, things are so drastically different that I have to constantly remind myself that I am not interacting with adults. As a teaching artist, my classroom is full of well-spoken teenagers, whose responses, poems, and blatant activism make them seem like they are as adept as some of my peers. But I am 29 going on

30, and some of the young women in my courses are 17 going on Jane Fonda with a hint of Sally Ride.

I've had the pleasure to share the stage with women I never thought I would meet but long looked up to, women who are older than me, well-accomplished, and have advice on how to run a Fortune 500 company and balance babies on their hips while doing so. Jade Iovine was someone who surprised me altogether. This 17-year-old trailblazer had claimed a spot in my long-term memory right alongside the time I sat next to Sandra Day O'Connor backstage at the Minerva Awards. Jade Iovine took a top seat on my list of people to watch, of women to admire.

Jade had seen me perform at the Minerva Awards with Maria Shriver. I had recently agreed to work with her father's headphone empire, Beats by Dr. Dre, when producer Sandy Glysteen called me in January 2012, to ask if I would consider performing at a young women's conference in Brentwood, California.

The phone rang at 11pm EST on a Sunday night, after I had just gone to bed. I woke and answered it, to hear Sandy say, "Hello doll, two words: Jade. Iovine." I responded with something like "bless you," or some other phrase to signify that I had no clue what she was talking about. She went on to tell me about this 17-year-old girl who had created a conference at her school titled "It's Our Turn." At this point, my personal life had taken a few sharp turns for the worst, and I was in no position to say "yes." And yet, I couldn't say "no."

Soon after, Jade and I had a chance to speak over the phone. I asked her why she wanted to do this. What I remember most about her response was her gorgeous honesty. She wanted an opportunity to tell girls her age that you didn't have to wait to make a difference, that you could start a revolution today, tonight, the afternoon after the event. The title of the conference suddenly seemed so fitting to me. I said "yes" and accepted the commission.

... ll--—»

Guest speakers at the conference included Raven-Symoné, Mary J. Blige, Alex Morgan, and Jess Weiner to name a few. Oh, and special guest Lady Gaga. I was honored to be on the playbill with such impressive talent and change makers.

When I sat in the audience after my morning panel and performance, it felt as if I was witnessing an adolescent who echoes a Joan of Arc spirit, housed in a 5'5" petite body, talking to a pop icon as if they went way back, in a comfortable yet respectable tone, like cashmere. Jade's line of questioning, intrigue in the responses of her celebrity guests, and her quiet command when no one was looking, reminded me of clips I had seen of stoic women, the kind who are antique now.

The day of the conference, I remember reflecting on my time in high school, my motives and thoughts. I was worried about the dance, not sharing a couch with Maria Shriver, not candidly speaking to Mary J. Blige, not empowering my generation to stop trying to heal bullying but how to deal and brace yourself for it. I wasn't talking to a poet at 10pm to commission a poem about the girls who only thought enough of themselves to be a well-dressed harlot after dark.

Times have changed, and this generation is pushing the envelope. Seems like more often than not, I am re-evaluating my impact, wingspan, and motives, checking to make sure I too am not accepting "no" as the easy and final answer.

And my students call me their instructor. If they only knew where I take my cues from.

 OUR TURN

Commissioned by
Jade Iovine for
It's Our Turn Conference

....

What if I told you, that I'm sorry you had to be the girl at the party who was dubbed the after-hours hoe? This nickname would never make your family proud. But I'm sure you have your adolescent reasons. For those of you pointing the finger, causing young women to change schools four times after the 8th grade, congratulations on entering the unfulfilling ranks of bullies. There is no pride there.

What if I begged you to believe that there isn't a difference in you and me, never mattered that you came from Pacific Palisades and I from suburban Crossroads.

If I said that this time in your life is the last time you will be this honest and that I hope you never experience the heartbreak of not realizing you could

change the world until you were 5.
Would you believe me?

Well, I couldn't decide what to say,
once I spoke to some 15 thousand
women who ranged from 40 to 60,
told them that I too believed in the
dream they benched when they were
your age, and you would hear the
emotion, relief, and realization.

I couldn't figure out if I was going to
stand here today and hope that you'd
just listen, even your mother dragged
you here. I am talking to you. And I am
hoping that someone today will pique
your interest. Yes you, Brentwood,
Harvard Westlake, Malibu, Poly Tech, or
Sierra Canyon.

Would you believe me if I told you that
someday I might run out of steam and
the Jess Weiners of the globe might
take some time off, what if someone
isn't ready to replace Jade or Mary J. or
Maria? Will you be ready to grab the
torch—without running from the calling
of changing the world?

I'm telling you now, it is your turn. Prove
this world wrong, 'cause folks think you
are apathetic, think that all you can
focus on is social status and class and just
defy the belief that you are more than

I love you text messages and pointless
status updates.

Prove me wrong, don't resist the urge to
go against the grain.
To not place your hand over your heart,
swearing to bliss that you are not a
well-dressed feminist. A feminist is a
compliment, not a life sans men, sans
sexy, sans striking. It is not a hard nose
pit bull-like energy dying to wear a suit
and tie just to get someone's attention.

Haven't you ever heard of Joan of Arc,
Sandra Day O'Connor, Coco Chanel or
Oprah Winfrey?

I have said it before, feminists wear
pearls and gowns to black tie affairs
and adorn boardrooms that are used to
brute colognes. This is not a new thing,
the waters have been charted for you to
navigate with grace.

What I am asking is, are you ready to
change the game? 'Cause everyone is
waiting to see your spark, time is passing,
and we are getting older.
So I'd like to know that someday later,
when I have no more poems to write,
when she has no more bills to pay,
goals to kick, history to make, that you,
the girl from the after-party dubbed
the infamous "hoe after dark" that

everyone can't stop updating their status about, place your hand over your heart, reaching past the superficial, and say, "Yes, it's my turn."

--o--

YOUR WORLDLY CLASSROOM, LOVE LETTERS & HANNAH

» *I never knew that a girl named Hannah would be intrinsically responsible for this Los Angeles native moving to her childhood fantasy home of New York City.*

From the first time I Skyped Hannah Katy in March 2011, I knew we would be friends. It felt instant, like two children in kindergarten sharing a love for castles in the sandbox during recess. We got along famously. Hannah was conducting my interview for shesthefirst.org, on our upcoming National Poetry Month partnership. The interview was a mixture of laughs, love of poetry, and talk of humanity. It was certainly one of the most effortless, enjoyable interviews I've ever had. The poetry workshop we had planned in Brooklyn was going to be amazing. If this interview was a sign, then I was in for a cupcake of a time.

It wasn't until April 28, 2012 that I found out that Hannah was the one who brought the idea of celebrating Poetry Month to raise money for girls' education to She's the First. Shaking my head, I thought to myself, "You think you had the whole story..."

Hannah and I became fast friends over a love for language, living, poems and Grey's Anatomy. We stayed closely linked through status updates and Gmail chat. It would be over a year before we met in person, in November 2011. I met her at a tea shop near Columbus Circle, and we embraced, as if we had lost touch after college, or that she moved away from our childhood neighborhood, but never as if we had just met. It was the kind of hug that says, "It's so good to see you, it's been forever." In essence, it had never been. In times such as these, I think social media has got to be the most epic thing to happen since God created the earth.

After tea, we had a Thai food dinner with Tammy Tibbetts of She's the First, and we sat at a table talking about how we were going to celebrate National Poetry Month the following year. We also talked about love lives, the lack thereof, love letters being left in the park all over the country, and the tweets that had changed our lives.

... / -—- / ...

Months later, in March 2012, Hannah came to stay with me in my Brooklyn brownstone. On that weekend, my world had just shattered, again. This happened to be the same weekend that we were going to read, edit, and assemble the anthology from 8,000 voices who sent us explicit poems about the world being their classroom.

The night before the editing began, I cried for what had seemed like days. I watched Hannah eat and never missed my appetite. I read Hannah poems that I had written when I wasn't heartbroken.

We talked until it was an hour past midnight. We spoke about the beauty of prayer, the dawn, love letters, and knowing better. If there was a camera crew there that night, onlookers would have bet that we were friends from the sandbox. But we had just met a few months prior.

Hannah answered a call to leave her loneliness inside of a letter affirming a woman she didn't know on the subway. She was now sitting Indian style on my rug, trying to convince me that mourning would end, that morning would be here soon, and that at some point, I'd stop crying.

The next day we read, and read, and read. I recall thinking, "well at least I am not the only one that is broken." The most common phrases in the submissions were centered on beauty, boys, heartbreak, sitting up straight, and very little about clean water, astronauts, and awkward-girls- turned-Millennial powerhouses.

If someone told me I could teach all the girls in the world, I wouldn't tell them that they are beautiful. I wouldn't tell them to watch their posture. I'd tell them that they won't look camera ready after 2 days of no sleep campaigning for hunger relief, and that is okay.

I would tell them that they should take more walks. I would tell them to get more friends named Hannah and Tammy. I would beg them to align themselves with a cause that was bigger than heartbreak. I would tell them that they will be fine, and afternoons will be spent laughing again. But I had been guilty of giving the same accolades and compliments on looks. This particular weekend, I had never felt so unattractive. One would have thought that 7,800 compliments and affirmations from women I may never meet would lift my spirits. But I just found myself going to the bathroom often to cry.

The poem following this narrative would be the first commission I had given myself. I wanted to write a response back to the seven or eight thousand people whose words I had the pleasure of reading on a weekend where I might have tried to end my own life for the hell I had placed myself in. This commission would be a poetic response to tell anyone listening that, "No, you are not beautiful," and "Yes, that is okay."

I don't know if I got a chance to personally thank her, for sitting beside me, while I pulled myself in and out of sobbing. She didn't ask me any questions, she just let me read, just offered napkins from the take-out she ordered for me to wipe my cheeks. At some points, I could feel her praying for me.
Hannah, it made all the difference. Thanks for being a love letter in human form.

//-—-//

»» NO, YOU'RE NOT (BEAUTIFUL)

Commissioned by
Azure Antoinette for
If the World Were My Classroom —
Voice Your Verse Campaign

....

I have never felt that way
just call me passable, plain, or
acceptable
'cause I don't know what to do with
the beauty
I used to revel in the way that the
word felt in my mouth, tongue
throwing it around outside to those I
thought deserved it
the word "beautiful" evokes reaction,
gives validation, and fills the voids that
the past left behind

what if, I believed it

that if every time someone
complimented my appearance, telling
me how grandiose my looks were/how
much impact is in my wingspan/that
I could change the world/demanding

that I sit straight because I am a
woman and we were born to carry on
the human race;
I have to wonder what I would have
accomplished by now

single handedly
I have yet to be an a relationship that
doesn't end poorly
constantly chasing the dream of
dreaming
praying to God, when I sometimes
think my prayers never reach Heaven,
the right path has a hard time
impressing me, and I have always
known better.
I wonder, if I was the woman who so
many told me I was, what I'd have to
revel in now

yes, call me passable then.
I'd rather be someone that you pass in
a metropolis where vanity is key
I'd rather stand behind the camera,
then try to focus my unwieldy
insecurities in front of it
yes, passable suits my feeling better

be honest with me
tell me that I am not beautiful, it's
okay
tell me that it's fine to not be thrilled
with my outward appearance
'cause you happen to find my mind

handsome
tell me that when I speak, you think
it's graceful
encourage me to believe that the way
I walk isn't awkward, it's winsome
don't call me generic
don't tell me that I am beauty
save that
for the weight of the word 'Friend'
after MySpace and Facebook stole its
meaning
you should chastise me
about wanting a good follower ratio
on twitter
when really I should only be worried
about following Christ

I'm sorry, never been good with
compliments, so you'll have to excuse
me
it's just that, I'd rather my intelligence
be bewitching
than to woo you with these lips that
have before told lies of confidence

I have trouble trusting
run after kind who paid me cents of
attention
that I converted into some twist of
undying affection
and that is a plight I could never be
proud of

at best, outwardly, I have felt passable

but have been lauded, told I have a
stunning personality
the ability to appear luminescent in a
dark space
so that has gotten me everywhere

and as any girl would
I've always wanted to feel ravishing,
drop dead, exquisite and in some '70s
complex sort of way, foxy
but I settled for poems/peaces of my
mind that never judged me/the ability
to place periods where I please
or
no punctuation at all

at the end of it, I'd love to settle with
being attractive
but, I have to be more than a word
more than a hopeful reflection in
societal crystalline mirrors
that reflect a being that I have trouble
reconciling with in the morning

and as for "beautiful," I'll take the
compliment later, when I have little
life left
when my face has more wrinkles than
glycation can account for or when
my hands are too arthritic to hold
the Mont Blanc pen that my mother
passed down to me. I'll take it when
someone asks you about the impact
that young people have had on my

life—and following my reply you say
"beautiful"

but please don't call me that as I
descend a staircase/not mid twilight/
not when you have to fill the infinite
silence—I won't believe you

as for "beautiful"—let me prove
myself to be awarded with that word
that was the intention, before we
sullied it with mediocrity

look, if there is dawn, then there are
new mercies at the beginning of it
it isn't too late, to exercise your
vocabulary
let me allure, arrest, and possess your
eyes, if only for a moment by what I do

just, make me work for it, I do
I want to be beautiful, but I still have
work to do yet
for today, that is good enough,
passable, acceptable

--o--

EAST COAST, WISDOM & MISTAKES

» *My best friend is a diehard LA Dodgers fan. She used to hate my key ring because it was a Yankee lanyard.*

Anyone who knows me would tell you I was always obsessed with the East Coast. Why, I couldn't really say, most likely it was because of the distance, the abrasion, and all of the lights. It seemed like a challenge, and the people I met from New York captivated me every time without fail.

.../ -—/ ...

During the morning greeting, or say-hello-to-the-new-visitor-time at my church in Los Angeles, I had the pleasure of meeting one of the associate pastors, Alex Pineda. He had recognized me from my brief appearances in HBO's Brave New Voices. I was one of the coaches for the Los Angeles team. The times my face flashed on camera were brief, small like the Keebler elves. So, it always made me laugh to have this claim to fame.

Alex and I ended up talking at the pastor's house one week, when he and his wife told me how much they loved the show, the work, the poets, and kids. I loved all the same things, so it brought a smile to my face.

Alex then told me he had arranged a stage reading of a biography he'd written, and he wanted me to perform on opening night.

I remember talking with Alex a few times on the days leading up to the show. We were both fairly busy and there had not been time to square away the specifics of the commission. In this line of work, I have learned that listening to the stories of the people who request the commissions is my greatest source of inspiration. I do not find inspiration in corporate content, annual reports, or press releases. I am usually very sensitive to the back story, the "why," or the emotional vision behind the concept.

I remember asking Alex what he was looking for. He told me he didn't want me to talk about the book. He didn't want me to tell his story in a truncated fashion via spoken word. He asked me to tell the story of the things I wish I knew when I was younger. What did I wish someone had told me? What are the lessons that I learned as a result of not having these conversations laced with wisdom and advice?

This was going to be an interesting poem. There were so many things that I did and still do wrong. How do I say all that I wish I knew in a two-to-three minute poem? I kept thinking that I would love to talk to someone now, someone who is 40 or 50, who will tell me wise things that will make the last decade sting less. My adolescence was marred with me moving too quickly, too many different faces the morning after, velvet stanchions, hazy Sunday brunches where I wore my sunglasses long after the sun had set. What was I going to say to young people, when I too felt 16. I had no choice but to sit myself in front of a mirror and be as honest as I could bear.

It was going to be painful, not deep, not lyrical, not uplifting. But it was something that I wanted to do, and hopefully some young person would listen and find the wisdom in my mistakes.

It felt risky and honest. It felt like the East Coast. And of course, Alex was from Jersey. Of course.

//----//

»» MARRIED TO THE PROMISE

Commissioned by
Alex Pineda

....

There are days, where I don't feel like
there are any more Indian summers
and days that I wish I could take back
my virginity from a world that raped
me of my innocence.
Mornings that I considered whiskey
with no apple juice chaser and it
would be great if I could stand here
and tell you that I was in my late
twenties, but I was a sophomore in
high school then.

Things were catastrophic by 16,
reprehensible by 21, and by 25, I had
years on my body that didn't translate
to my face, so I smiled instead and
replied "fine" when asked how I was.
I got good at massaging the truth to
suit my denial.

I fell to my knees for the wrong
reasons, always the wrong persuasion.
I found vices in bottles and skin and I

would love to tell you that now, things are golden; I would love to tell you that now I want for nothing.

But I owe you the truth, owe you whiskey with no chaser, so I will tell you that these days, I pray every time I forget my salvation, I stay away from clubs, 'cause I know the power of bass and shots; there is no happy ending for me with establishments that call barstools furniture.

So here we are, present day, I have kicked the habit of calling home to alcoholic libations, and spend my nights alone when it is time to close my eyes. If I had a younger me that I could spit wisdom to, I would tell her that this road isn't easy. I would tell her that she should be nice to her mother, 'cause frankly that is all the family she's got. I would tell her that she is going to burn through relationships as quickly as society discards celebrities that don't make tabloids.

I'd tell her not to get jaded, that people do stay married and that you don't have to cheat to keep spice in a relationship, I'd tell her that role play is for theatre. I'd tell her that people are going to demand that she keeps her head up and that she will be trying to claw her way up from rock bottom, I'd tell her that her self-worth would be compromised and she in turn would compromise herself. I'd beg her not to go to that party that the seniors were throwing, because that is where she would be raped.

I'd tell her, if you are going to be on your knees, it better be to pray and not 'cause you are trying to prove your maturity in a world that never wanted you to be a child first. You get married to the promise that things will inevitably be okay, and they will. I'd tell her that she will be fine, but it will all hurt, and sometimes she will have to remind herself of good things. I'd tell her that she just may think that the world has gone black and she can't afford to pay for enlightenment.

I'd tell her that you are going to end up a poet, and your life is going to provide you material. I would tell her not to worry, 'cause all that she is going to endure, God sees. And God will give you stanzas 'cause he knows that life that you will lead.

...][...

THE HUMAN CONDITION

...][...

SOCIAL NETWORKS, LCD SCREENS & VIRAL HUMANITY

» *Understanding social media was a gradual process for me.*

I remember talking about how trivial MySpace was, and then before long, I had an account with more than 1,000 friends. Then I recall watching the rise of Facebook and signing up for this background-less, need-not-be-savvy-in-HTML social network, then throwing myself into the crashing waves of Twitter, wondering why people were constantly using the pound sign in front of words.

I have come a long way, now at any given moment, I have three websites to discuss my day, the lunch I did or did not have, and talk about the Yankees winning the World Series. Today, thinking about all the self-promotion we do is somewhat laughable, and then sad, and then depressing. I have to pacify myself by saying the reason I have Twitter and Facebook is because my line of work requires the public presence. I tell myself that if I were not a performance artist and arts advocate, I wouldn't be on the networks, I'd treasure my anonymity.

Or would I? Being born in this era is something for which I forget to be grateful. Watching people of my mother's generation or listening to my grandmother talk about getting the "interweb," so that she can dive online, is hysterical to me. Often I sleep with my laptop, wake up to 20 downloaded email messages on my iPhone, respond to the six that aren't spam, prioritize the text messages that need a reply, all before I place my feet on the floor to get up. I know this isn't healthy, but I don't know how else to operate. The fear that I had as a child of "missing something" has returned, except this time, it is masked with a glowing LCD. I am addicted to being plugged in, panic creeps in when my phone nears 30 percent, because I know battery death is eminent. I always think, what if the call that I didn't know I was waiting for goes automatically to voicemail, or the email commission of a lifetime has to wait for me to read it until I can plug into a power source? And what happens if once I have plugged in, they have found a different poet and I will have missed my chance?

More and more, I am realizing that your destiny is specifically for YOU—it cannot be captured by someone who isn't you. Learning this lesson each time I start to panic is helpful, however, I would love the learning to convert to my memory, and when the phone dies, when the laptop is out of reach, to remember that the opportunity of a lifetime is for my lifetime, that the voicemail will kindly ask me to call whomever is inviting me back at my earliest convenience, and the email replies will wait until I have at least had a moment to thank God for waking me up to see another day.

.../ -—-/ ...

I realized a few years ago that our humanity was going mute—it was transitioning to 140-character emotions, confessions that we could give the world via status updates, yet stare at our loved ones with closed mouths, filling rooms with void. Laughing at a timeline had replaced enjoying a dinner out with your family. I was sending e-bouquets of flowers to my mom on Mother's Day. Sending birthday greetings to my 1,000 friends on Facebook, 700 or 800 of whom I had never met, was standard. This was the new regular and I was on the train with no intention of getting off.

In 2008, I wrote the poem that changed my view of how I saw myself in the wake of this technology age. The Executive Director of a Los Angeles-based arts organization asked me to write a poem about the desensitization of our culture. At first, I thought it was an interesting concept, the laptop/Blackberry obsession was in full swing for me. But I wasn't sure how I was going to be authentic when I am clearly part of the society that think computers do it best...that is, until my heart breaks, and I actually need a hug, a handwritten note, or a shoulder to lean on. Computers can't do that, Skype can't convey the acceptance of holding a hand, or touching a face.

I took this commission as a chance to see the world, including myself, from a perspective that wasn't judging or condemning, just acknowledging that this is where we are. In evaluating the state of affairs that my own life was in, I was able to write about the tragedy of humanity going viral. I have performed this poem all over the country, and every time it ends, I am approached by so many people, young and old, who share my sentiment, who sleep with their Macs, depend on their cellular devices to transmit the purpose in their lives, and people who forget to take their mom a potted plant on a random Thursday and instead send her an e-card via Hallmark. com on Mother's Day. One commission turned into two, which spawned a speaking topic titled "The Human Condition." To date, I have traveled to 10 or more conferences, opening my lecture with Humanity or Global Conversation, and I follow the poem up with an invitation for attendees to join in a discussion about where we are, where we are going, and how we manage this digital implosion.

Every time I start the following poems, I feel like I am taking a risk, blaming myself for not being a better human, and by the end of the poem, I feel exposed. I am thankful for the transparency and the willingness of those who have approached me after hearing them. It lets me know that I am not the only one with work to do. It lets me know that I am not the only one dying to be human again.

//-—-//

INNER VOICE

Commissioned by ICAN for the 2013 Women's Leadership Conference

....

As a woman I am constantly faced with trying to siphon the amount of emotion I place on situations, things, men, appearance, women that were never really my friends, and living in a world where I am trying to make sure that the word feminist, looks good on me.

I am consistently battling my femininity, my former self, and the woman I'd like to be paralleled with the woman I am currently. Which really just exhausts me. I used to be enough for myself in the morning, sufficient by the afternoon, reveled in play dates with my friends who hadn't learned how to be catty, we were too little to be superficial, and by the evening, I had already conquered being a heart surgeon, a top chef and according to my father, I was always a princess.

What did I do with my confidence?
Where did I misplace the wilds in me
that told me that anything I wanted to
accomplish could be done before my
mid-day nap?

I have been looking in all the wrong
places.
I have been searching for my identity
in pencil skirts that would look just
right, if my waist were a little tighter.
I have been searching for the fearless-
ness of my youth in cosmetics that sit
just right on cheekbones that have
been engineered by Photoshop
programs.
I have been looking for my purpose, in
desk placards, empowerment conferences, cherry wood desks that have a
view of the city.
I have been searching, long distances,
epic widths, for an answer, a piece
of validation, for the courage to be
myself.

As a little girl, I can remember, playing
with dolls, building sand castles, and
reveling in anything that was make-
believe.
I also fondly recall that there was a
voice inside of my chest that sounded
like a mature me.
She would tell me that I could do it,
that everything was possible.

She'd tell me that I could make a 3-tier
cake, on the beach, out of wet mud.
She would tell me that my mom would
think it was the best butter-cream
frosted, with ripe strawberries cake,
she had ever tasted.

I can remember this voice, whispering
to me right before I stopped fighting
sleep.
She would tell that tomorrow is going
to be epic.
That we are going to riches off of our
lost teeth that we placed underneath
my pillow, and that we were going to
wear a beautiful gown made of bed
sheets, she would tell me that the
household pet would be my loyal subject and we would rule the kingdom of
the neighborhood.
I would smile.

In the morning, it would be just as I
heard the night before.
This inner voice never lied to me.
But she stopped speaking to me at
some point, or maybe I just couldn't
hear it.
All I can confirm was that she was nowhere to be found.
She didn't come with me to college;
she wasn't there at my first official
staff meeting,
she wasn't there at 1am while I slaved

over my first PowerPoint, or the midnight when my son had vengeful fever
and I had a conference call in shanghai
at the same time.

But last night around 2am, when I had
lost all faith in myself, I heard someone
that sounded like me at 4 years of age.
I felt a tapping on the side of my chest,
near my heart, the tapping increased
to a moderate push.
Then the room fell quiet, the voice
said, it's me.
It's been a while, but I have never left
you, I know you are filled with worry,
but you can do this.

Tomorrow, you will wear a suit that is
just as nice as the bed sheets we used
to make your gowns out of.
And tomorrow you will realize your
dream.
And tomorrow we will turn the key in
the ignition.
Yes, tomorrow the flame will hit the
piston.
And tomorrow you will make this situation obey your desire.
And tomorrow you will conquer the
world that you live in.
And you will do it, before your mid-
day nap.
Tomorrow is the day to set the globe
aflame with your prowess.

I smiled, she told me to rest well, and
she told me to have a good evening
She whispered, tomorrow we ignite.

»» HUMANITY

Commissioned by ACFCLA for American Cancer Society Benefit — Art 4 Life

....

The tragedy is this:
The focus on family values is non-existent, reality shows raise children
and children are giving birth to babies,
and babies are being auctioned off
to the highest American bidder,
and Americans are wasteful, and
the Global Waste is billowing out of
smokestacks in neighborhoods that
have outsourced all the available
work to India where English is a third
tongue, and third worlds in my mind
are first and first I should have called
you I guess...
I should have called instead of
updating my status on social network
sites, no I am not well, yes I am
struggling, and maybe I will show up
tonight, I probably won't though,
because truth is I don't know if I have
enough gas to get back home and I
would never tell you that, because I

am dying to stay a poet and I am too
involved with my own self loathing to
genuinely ask you how you are.

How come?

What happened to the day's prior to
TiVo?
It must have vacated with the
serendipity of hugs
And left with the art of writing a
"thank you" note
Gone are the days of sitting in a
maroon parlor discussing comings
and going of current events...I
have not felt the grit of newspaper
soot between these digits, these
fingertips no longer have calluses from
Ticonderoga instruments, I Mac book
to keep things moving
And yet, I am still...
Gone are they, the days of coming by
with chicken noodle
Now I would rather send you an
e-caldron of broth via Facebook

Where did the time go?

When it was wax emblems on
parchment
Inside detailing the details of everyday
life
Purchases, deaths, marriage, birth,
longing, lust, monotony and kindness

Mornings aren't what they used to be
No Folgers misty awakenings with
terry cloth robes in tow
Now the best part of waking up is red
bull monster and a five-hour energy
shot in your cup.

So, where did we go?

When did we replace sanity with
insatiable
When did we say
Humanity you need to sit in the back
and let mass consumerism drive
Or,
Consciousness please recede and
cognizance take heed.
It is time for ATMs and mp3s to
determine human worth...

But I should tell you
I have no humanity left
I am guilty of not stopping to smell the
dandelions
I haven't taken my hands out of my
pockets to give a hand out in some
time.
I text before I speak in the morning,
the dawn is interrupted from the
illumination of my cell phone (I know
that God is upset with me)
I would love to tell you that I would be
reformed
Regain a remnant of compassion and

find a human thread by the end of this
poem

But Rome wasn't built in a day, and
America, it took hundreds of years to
build the reputation that we discover
lands that were already inhabited
And I don't know if I will be human
again in time to end this poem
But I give you my poetic word that I
am dying to live again.

and just be.

--o--

IT TAKES A VILLAGE

» »

Commissioned by ACFCLA
for "It takes a Village Concert"

. . . .

(Melody)

Kiss dawns
feet crush embers from fires
from night prior
man child Strolling along coastline
Climbing amongst evergreens and
palms with no name
In the village
It is morning
like the Nile, quiet
adolescent queens
Gather bushels
pomegranates, bananas, Jamaica, husk
and straw
Infants strapped to back
Laundered sheets keep the Zions and
Sheebas of the world safe
Listen
Distant hymns of Congo
Chants of Tutsis
Scent of Shamans

in the village
its morning

(Melody)

Misty manholes
Traveled by Cole Haan soles and crocks
There is work to be done
Oshkosh harnesses
Keep the Shilohs and Suris
of the world safe
Hear the Velcro of holstered cell
phones
the being sliced by soccer balls
In the city its morning
Time for trade, stock and
consummation
time for education
Population of the mind
Never mind the antiquated thought of
ignorance being bliss

It's not
It takes a village
Whether you dance, pray
play, sing, or stray
It takes you
changing and altering
holding one another
Touch palms
Kiss grandmothers
wash indiscretion clean
sins float upon the Atlantic
it is time to iron creases

Of deceased loved ones

It takes a village
Of metro, ghetto, tribe
gated, jaded, enterprise
privilege cul-de-sac
and
no gender bias

Take sons of abusive fathers
daughters born independent
Children rejected
Parents willing to pick up the slack

It takes a village
city, it's morning
village, it's morning

It takes a village

(Melody)

Takes a village to change.

» » GLOBAL CONVERSATION: THE BEGINNING

Commissioned by ICAN Global & Create the Space You Deserve

....

How could you possibly feel attached, connected to the person sitting next to you?

When you have no idea what smells make them smile and remember the good things in life?

There were times when things were simpler and we waited to get home to check the messages on the rectangle box that would blink.
Now, there is always a way to contact one another, and you would think that we could stand to rid ourselves of voicemail. Certainly between Twitter, Facebook, LinkedIn, and a monochromatic Outlook, there is no need to talk after the beep.

Just so we are clear, the human

condition as we know it, has gone viral.

However, in a rural place without the efficiency of technology, there is still a belief that you are so much more than the last four digits of your social security number. Even though that is the only way you can validate your identity and the systems on the phone won't let you access your personal information if you can't tell the customer service rep in India your mother's first teacher's name.

I know, dross, right?

Everyone is looking for something, someplace where we still find value in speaking face to face, someplace where hands still meet and warmth is generated from salutations. Perhaps, that is what brought you here. You too are looking to create the space you deserve.

It is less about the problem, more about interconnectedness—on a global divide, hurt and heartache is the same in Burma as it is in Manchester. Love feels the same in Sudan and Stockholm; goose bumps have the same texture in Omaha as they do in Orlando.

The point for today is that you leave
here different than when you came in.
Leave this place imparting and parting
wisdom to a society that has lost hope
and can't spell out the whole word
"beacon" without be concerned of
character limits.

Today is a start—a covenant between
you, God, and Andromeda.
change is necessary.
Just the other night, Orion's Belt
whispered to a shooting star,
"Remember when everyone used to
gaze in our direction?"
The constellations miss all of us
looking up and wishing—fountains
don't often see the coins they used
to, because we keep a wish list in our
phones.

Convenience is a gift, but midnight
conversations over earl grey and
chocolate cake are rare gemstones that
are close to extinction.

Between you and I, I will admit it first.
I indeed have a problem—I am taking
the first step in saying that I don't
really remember whispers and "when
I grow up" conversations. In truth I
do not know what to do with these
muscles in my face when I catch
someone catching my eye, so I just wince.

I am desperate to feel a human
sensation—I swear I am.

They say that before you walk, you
must crawl, so I guess we can start with
kindergarten—start with the basics.

I will put my phone on silent and turn
my humanity on loud.

Please just tell me about yourself, what
makes your skin ripple and when you
were little, did you used to want to
change the world?

Yea, me too.

»» GLOBAL CONVERSATION: WHAT NOW?

*Commissioned by ICAN Global
& Create the Space You Deserve*

....

There is a brokenness about the
human spirit
to startle is not the intention, to sting
is not the hope.
To Stun—that is what is needed.
I know that things move quickly
but there isn't time for a nervous
breakdown
this meeting has little to do with
convenience

Question your inner self; the one
that used to dream about ridding
indifference.
What now?
What you do with the information?
Who can I call, you say—who will hear
my cry—there is no apathy in me.

Whether or not you have answers to

the aforementioned is moot, however, what you do with the information you have received is entirely up to you.

I would caution you to remember that it all matters.

As far as the looming question of what now, what can I do in my home, office, shift, small group, fellowship, corridor, and community? Relax, take a deep breath—you don't have to touch two million, five lives is enough.

Again, you ask, what now—as mediocre settles into crevices, I say—
Lose it.
Well-behaved women have never made history. Remember Joan of Arc, Minerva, Jane Austen, Cleopatra, Marie Curie, or Amelia Earhart and Anne Frank.
I say, "to the underworld," with "safe" and "knowing one's place."

Where are you going now, what is your destination tonight, I caution you to think about each solitary movement that you make. I am no soothsayer, have no crystal, but you just may be what the globe needs. We are past the desperate need of a kiss on the forehead and a pat on shoulder blades, just to assure all of us that it

189

will be okay.

At this point, you are probably focused
on reflection, someone told you an
amazing story of triumph and you
were so happy to be impacted that
the slightest sentiment brings tears
to your eyes. No one remembers the
mundane, but hearts all over the globe
recall a kind word, there is an essence
in receiving a hug, a solidarity in a
handshake, and honesty in telling the
truth when someone ask you how you
are—answer simply.

Right now, your focus is splitting
follicles 'cause its time to pick up
your children, make dinner, create
a new spin on an effective merger,
or whatever is consuming your mind
that has been reduced to one track.
But inside your chest is a heart that is
begging you to stay in the mode of
this think tank, like minds and ready
spirits.
But now what do you do with
the emotional saturation, the
"overwhelm," the application of
changing the world.

All you want to do is abandon the
mediocrity of living without purpose.

If you are here—you ALREADY HAVE.

The courage that it took to bring you
this Global Conversation says that you
know that we can't do this without
you. That this world is desperate for
your gift and you ARE appreciated,
your efforts are lauded. Don't give
up, never give in to the notion that 70
percent is the new 100. You are better
than that. It is time for an adjustment,
it is time to create the space you so
desperately deserve.

Change is not only uncomfortable, it is
eminent.

--o--

POEM ON THE FLY

Commissioned by
the Association Forum
of Chicagoland

....

Creativity and Connection are large words—not in the multi syllabic sense, but in the heft they hold. And to ask a person what refreshes them and expect an answer that isn't a status update merely defies the odds.

Because when you hear creativity you think about seeing things differently—you think about the box that they tell you to think outside of, and I wonder what it must be like to be the actual box, if in fact we all followed suit—then that very carton would insurmountably lonely. This world, runs on all kinds—some that are box dwellers, some that see it as a cardboard mansion for those who consider themselves homeless and thrive in the world unsheltered.

I think it all takes courage, the kind

that hugs you close and let's you know
that it is ok to be different, the kind
of courage that lives in the open mind
—the brain that has no bounds—the
organ that views the universe as minia-
ture. But it takes an enormous amount
of stomach to attend a conference, to
be more than the characters that fit
on your name badge, to stay passionate, when there is only deadline, only
meetings with no resolution and the
sight of a changing wind doesn't fit in
the budget.

It takes an enormous amount of
stomach to answer the questions on
intimidating white boards that stand
as tall as you used to feel to answer
questions like "how do you connect
with the world around you?" At first
sight, I get down on myself, but you
anonymous courage keeper answered
back "through laughter". You that I
may never meet; said that you connect
through social media, through pick-
ing up your phone and checking in,
through volunteering, through making
an effort to talk face to face.

And here I am, worried about an inbox
—I too, forget to laugh, to find the
joke in the massacre. But here—in this
Midwest place that plays wind songs
that some call hurricanes, we can

candidly talk openly about fear, about what refreshes you and why?

And I never thought it would take a room full of association professionals to remind me to relax, to travel not for work, to sleep, breathe, and give yoga another try. Someone said that "patios" refresh them, and another responded with "weekends", but the one that stuck out to me was the word "hug". I could use one, from maybe you, maybe you.

Thank you for the honesty—people I may never meet, and to the one that wrote "I don't do this very well"—you are doing great, thank you for the courage, thank you for being honest, I don't do that well all the time either, but its fine—moment to moment.

MEDICINE

(not like the kind on tv)

PATIENTS, PATIENCE & PRACTICE

» *I was getting used to my new job, if you can call it that.*

On any given Tuesday, I was talking to young people about the Eminem mastering the art of inner rhyme, or flying to Brooklyn to meet a group of young women that were going to defy the odds of inner city and make it through a four-year college. I had gotten used to not admiring Saturdays, because for me Thursdays were just as good, and most often Mondays were quiet – not stressful, not full of regret. I can remember loathing Sundays, because it meant the weekend was coming to an end and I would have to go back to work.

Since I made the decision to pursue the arts full time, I looked forward to every day, I had to, the entertainment profession is chalk full of rejection. When I got the call from my agency to write two commissioned poems for the Planetree Annual Conference I felt blessed to receive new work and it had started to feel routine, I was finding my groove and slowly paying off the enormous debt I had incurred in the last 7 years.

My agent Brenda was telling me about the work this particular client does, Planetree specifically is a network of medical facilities, practices, residential care, and hospitals that pride themselves on being Patient Centered. Meaning, they push to keep the patient, the focus – as opposed to the pharmaceutical quotas, billing bureaucracy and other components that contribute to the PNL.

This was an interesting concept for me to grasp, once I left corporate America, I left the benefits as well. I had no health insurance, and after leaving the consistency of full time employment, two of my back teeth had broken in half, I had become a frequent visitor of my OB/GYN for ovarian cysts that wanted to mimic cancer, and had a violent attack of vertigo that we most recently discovered was Multiple Sclerosis according to the county ER physician. Naturally, this all occurred once my health insurance expired. During each medical crisis that warranted me seeking professional help. I rarely felt like I was center, more the outcast.

Once I recovered from the realization that I had no insurance as a result of pursuing a passion, I adapted, as many artists do. I discovered self medicating remedies that would keep me in the race, kept Orajel with me at all times, took copious amounts of Motrin and favorited WebMD on my laptop. I knew I needed medical assistance, but "insurance ain't for poets".

In the many doctors offices, emergency rooms and clinics I have visited, I can safely say that the overall energy of the staff immediately shifts once you have declared that you have no health insurance. Suddenly everything is outpatient, paid in full prior to procedure, or exponential residual billing can be counted as a certainty.

So if this Planetree focused on the person, and not the fact that the patient was a poet, who was trying to not contract a stress disorder for lack of loving her life as an adult, I was intrigued. I, wanted to know more. The Annual Conference was open to all participants of the Planetree network, this included surgeons, nurses, VA staff, hospice workers, cafeteria managers, and orderlies.

Other than my connection to medical dramas on TV I had no unifying prose for people in this industry. I remember going to doctor appointments with my mother and as a child wondering why they couldn't "fix" her. I don't understand medicine, I don't understand why something as necessary as this profession is to any living human being is called Practice.

I am constantly reminding myself to be careful where I place my faith, telling myself that I fall short, that I fail people, disappoint them, that I am human. In being human, people will fail me as well, disappoint me because they are no different than you and I. Often I forget that doctors, nurses, and care workers are human too. We are the same, we both write poems, I with words while they use sutures, scalpels and methodical diagnosis.

As human beings we will make mistakes, over look the obvious because of fatigue, and err not always on the side of caution. The difference is, that the people in the medical profession are responsible for the vitals of all the people that we love. So, there is no room for mistakes, fatigue, erring on the side of caution or disappointment. Oversights are malpractice suits, and a doctor operating on 2 hours of sleep in 2 days will ultimately end in negligence, whereas some may call that insomnia or a great weekend.

——»+++

Planetree took 4 days out of the year to invite their patient centered network to a conference that would recharge them, remind these life maintainers of why they made a decision to answer the call of medicine. Planetree had decided to commission a poet to open and close this recharging conference. Once I understood the task, I could only manage to feel overwhelmed.

What would I say to hotel banquet room of medical professionals, do I say thank you for saving my mom? Do I say, thank you for looking out for my aunt in chemotherapy, do I tell them that I don't understand how I can teleconference with someone in Beijing that I have never met in person and yet Cancer is still stealing memories that have yet to be made from families all over the world. I couldn't help not getting overly emotional. Thinking how terrified I was to be 28 years old and not have the ability to hold a paper plate still, I thought about when I lost the ability to walk while strolling to the bank on Hollywood and Vine and when my mom took me to the emergency clinic the doctor told us both that I was stressed — he advised me to take an anti-inflammatory and call the office in 2 weeks to update them on my progress. No one seemed to care that I felt like there was a vice grip around my chest and breathing seemed optional. I wanted to undergo a large panel of testing, in my mind, I knew something was wrong but I didn't have insurance and further testing is expensive, I haven't written enough commissioned poems to pay for someone to evaluate why I didn't feel well. This was my reality; health care was a luxury, like education, like gated communities.

I felt like the practice of medicine had failed me, and now, I was being asked to remind the very doctors that I was losing faith in, to re-charge. Everything seemed to contradict in my mind at this time, I felt exhausted and I hadn't even begun to write.

For the second time since making the decision to pursue this passion of mine full time, I felt like saying "yes" was again hasty, possibly a mistake. I didn't know what to say to Planetree, to this network of patient centered caring human beings.

It wasn't until a group conference call that I felt the inspiration. There must have been 5 different voices, and although the 5 voices were from different departments, they had a unifying passion, their voices were filled with empathy, concern, all surrounding people like me, like my mom, and my sister, my aunt, friends and acquaintances—some who had lost the fight, to cancers and heart arrhythmias.

It seemed clear all at once. I couldn't talk to medical professions about their work, I could only talk to them as a patient, thank them for their patience and tell them that everyone is counting on you. That we, put our faith in the initials behind their last names, and to say thank you, for answering call from medicine and staying in the race.

On behalf of poets, mothers, in-laws, and all of the labels too numerous to mention, we say "Thank You", for showing up to practice. Our lives depend on it.

//-—-//

»» PLANE TREE

Commissioned by Planetree for the Annual Conference

....

In theory, hospital corners could be
more than an ornate way to make a
bed, just as much as bedside manner
has always been more than how
one acts by the side of the bed. But
patient-centered care means nothing
other than the patient is the nucleus,
the epicenter, of the proposed ailment.
When people think healthcare,
most would argue that the person
being cared for is paramount, when
the actual is to the contrary. This is
more than an actionable complaint.
But somewhere along the line,
the prescriptions took the place of
grandfather memories and sisterly
banter. Somewhere along the way, it
became less about maternity and more
about fiduciary gain.
My supposition is this.

I'm thankful that there is still majesty

for going rogue.

That in this nation, there are whole
facilities banded together under a
Robin Hood mentality, caring for
cancers that wear preliminary masks as
influenzas. I'm so elated that there are
facilities bandaging bypass and arterial
tears and masses and metabolic
myopathies, all while dressing feverish
tongues with ice chips. The thought
that my 25-year-old cancerous mother
or that man named Michael, my
Auntie Tonni, or stroke patient who
went by Sylvia, only to her friends, had
someone to ease their fears—gives me
hope for this sterile society.

Otherwise, I would have to resolve
that they had no one to caress the roof
of their quivering palms and whisper
"it's okay" to ear lobes that had grown
accustomed to bad news.

Truthfully, when I hear patient-
centered care, my ears hum a slow
bluegrass tune, and my eyes glaze over
to honey rhubarb like tone and I see
ice tea in canned jars on porches in
Nashville, Tennessee.
There things are real slow
people still ask how you do and
gentleman smell like aftershave
hold the door open

even if you have never acted like a lady.

Yes, there—time hasn't been
inundated with overwrought
efficiency—the trees are plain and
children stay young long enough to
really want to be Harry Potter on
Tuesday, veterinarian on Thursday,
but end up an international business
attorney that adores Tolstoy for light
reading in the end.

The revolution was never intended to
be televised, and patient-centered care
was the last thing that would have
been classified as a fad. For decades,
activists have cared quietly, avid but
respectfully quiet. As it stands, the
creed of America echoes equality
and justice for all. I have yet to read
any paragraph in those governing
documents about national healthcare.
I suppose the powers that were meant
for its inclusion in theory failed to
instill it in practice.

I can only wish that residential,
nursing, physician hospitals that were
patient-centered weren't pushed in
a corner. I wish that a place where
patients had center was enough to fill
an entire South Eastern hemisphere
and I say prayers for Judy with stage
4 melanoma and Melanie with

Huntington's and for Marty whose
dementia has taken the place of his
twins taking their first step.

Disease is a thief of all the things that
make us human, and we all just wish
for successful in vitro fertilizations—
explainable adoptions, stronger viral
loads, and careful immunizations that
don't backfire like H-bombs strapped
to the inside of failing immune
systems.

Humanity is going deaf to touch, and
emotion and and and—I just close my
eyes, thank the only God I know for
people in healthcare, people who still
love one another, for orderlies that
escort my now 62-year-old mother up
the handicap-enabled side ramp. I cry
at the thought of the doctors who
take extra moments they were never
granted to listen to possible first-step
stories, repeated fears, and lonely
suggestions, and each day I hold a
space in my heart for all the facets of
nursing cause that is how we all came
into the world—being nursed. We
were cradled into the atmosphere,
never wondering what human touch
felt like, never wondering what it must
be to be the center of a world that is
full of hospital, neat, sterile corners.
We never questioned warmth.

I never knew of such a place in my
conscious.
I would like to believe that I am well-
informed
but this decade lived three times over
must have caused
the quietest revolution—I know I
missed it.
As we all know, the revolution was not
meant to be televised.

Sometimes I daydream, head south
of where I reside—where things
are slow, there are Creamsicles that
conjure memory, aftershave, and
honey-flavored butter for warm
grandmother-baked bread, pure
love, fresh compliment, and the air
smells like a twist between brown
sugar and strawberries. There—I am
in the middle of the town square,
appreciating toddlers in espadrilles.
There—the experience is patient
centered, no matter the location.
Be that, nursing facility, physician or
long-term resident care, it's the same
emotion-filled experience. In my
dream, the breeze is gentle and there
is shade from the buoyant PlaneTrees.

--o--

»» REMEMBER.

Commissioned by Planetree for the Annual Conference

....

5, 10, 15, or 27 years ago, you had a dream.

At some point, the notions of astronauts and rock star left your lexicon—at some point, you decided to answer the call and join the ranks of care giving.

Today, CEOs share armrests with cafeteria employees, you both share a hankering for gambling and tables with terrible odds, and nurses and doctors become everything before the initials following their last names. Point being that you picked a profession that is called "the Lord's work" and this profession gladly welcomed you into this overwhelming cycle of mortality, memory loss, "there isn't enough time," and "she was too young."

Before I go on, I wanted to thank you for helping me adjust to my ailments and for spending a little extra time with your patients, their families, and researching that procedure when it just cleared clinical trials.

You should know, there will continue to be days that challenge your will to stay in this profession. Mothers will snap, fathers will grow verbose when they categorically have been silent. Life is short and from their perspective you hold bad news between your teeth. According to the families you work with, you are the only person standing between life and death.

It's heavy.

My recommendation as someone who isn't in your line of work is to grab a pebble. Remember the fond point when you answered the charge to do this. Purse your lips and remember the smell of your first textbook, recall the image of the professor that made you believe in the beauty of knowledge. Place the pebble in your palm center and hope. It's alright if you close your eyes. Just glaze your index finger over the ridges and breathe, exhaling the formality, inhaling the possibility.

You can do this, you can pay it forward. Try again.

You will go back to the hospital, hospice, administration office, janitorial post, and cafeteria position. The excitement will dwindle, the light fades. It is so paramount to remember how you feel right now. Hand over your chest, feel that, your heart is beating eight times its resting rate. That feeling is inspiration, that moisture in your palms has ascended to the surface because you have been awakened. Just think, the last time that you felt this way you were 15 or 22 or young enough to remember that memory that still brings you to tears. There was a reason you were chosen to be here amongst colleagues that could never handle the charge.

Let me ask you something. How do you want to be remembered? Not after death, I mean the minute you leave a present moment. What do people say when you leave the room, when you are done with your conversation? Do they feel your compassion, do they see the youthful courage that comes from toddlers in your eyes, do you reach them on a level that can only be felt by human touch? Or have you settled into the rigor of responsibility, mortgage, bureaucracy, and quota? It's alright, it happens—the auxiliary effects of being an adult.

However, this is your wake-up call, a last-minute charge from a poet who is counting on you all to make sure her mother understand the basics of arthritis, a daughter who is perplexed with all the questions of a young women diagnosed with MS. This is a plea from every patient you'll encounter for as long as the profession will hold you. We don't need jargon, medical-speak of lipids, levels, and laboratory results. We need smiles, complimentary physical therapy, the active listening, and the pause after the over-used "How are you today?"

Stay invested. Remember this heartbeat of yours, the blood coursing through your able veins, remember what brought you here, remember the pebble, remember the promise, forget the compromise and deadline and statistic. You are the key, humans caring for humans, you caring for me, me trusting you to help. The business of placing the patient in the center is an all-out war, an outcry for a society that thinks computers can do it best. This is you taking back the

reigns and pressing forward on the
revolution that was never intended to
be televised.

Straighten your back, inhale deep,
clear your throat, 'cause you are living.

--o--

WALK A DAY IN MY SHOES

>> >>

Commissioned by SEIU — LA Healthcare Workers Rally

....

walk a day in my shoes
an hour, a moment if that is all
your time will permit
in the soles you will feel
grit, coherence,
you will feel the determination
to stretch an 11 dollar hourly wage
into a small fortune of
free memories

now, pull the tongue
listen to the voices of a union
that doesn't tolerate its members not
having basic human rights
like the luxury of healthcare

tie the laces now
tight, tighter, hold them fast together
ball them in your fist and clinch
running is a stream of sweat
from two million workers that
work harder than most dream

AZURE ANTOINETTE ·

211

now rise to your heels
no doubt your feet are cramping
your calve muscles in atrophy
it is to be expected

the supplemental job you
must take makes your day
26 hours long and eight days for a
work week

your primary employment
is under the auspice
that healthcare is secondary

put your head back up
raise your weary eyes
and march, to the beat of
healthy hearts that are clamoring
for your success

open your mouth,
clear your throat
and inhale the smell of change
it takes like ginger, persimmon
and justice.

Nursing has been called the Lord's
work
so know you are then an angel,
march prophetic, prophet-like
carry the spirit of the fallen with you
hold your children's breath in your
mind
let the breeze carry the scent

of your spouse
inhale again, and remember why you
work
smile, even if your teeth
don't often glance at the world
know you are winning

tell your country
of what you learned as you strolled
in my path

tell America that the prize
is not modification loans
or renting to own, tell them not to
invest
in the fidelity of corporations that
may fail you

tell them not to retire funds in stock
with decent dividends, high yields, and
trusts
ask America to invest in me

so that when its citizens fall ill
when their citizens grow tired
I, a health care worker, can provide
your tongue with ice chips, your
stomach
with chicken broth, a sponge bath,
massage, triage, vaccination,
medication,
and a manner befitting a
bedside

I promise,
when you fall ill
I will take care of you
for now you can start
by asking America if she will take care
of me

when you are through
place my shoes back at my bedside
time is drawing nigh and soon
I must rise and begin another day

--o--

PREAMBLE, HANDSOME PILOTS & RECITATION

» *One of my first recitations was the Preamble to the Constitution.*

This was not a homework assignment for school, rather a requirement of my beloved mother. She believed the governing documents of the United States were filled with gorgeous language that one should be able to recite at a moment's notice.

At the time, I vehemently did not agree with her. I was eight years old, and nothing about men in white wigs, writing with pens that didn't have ball points, moved me. My mom, however, worked in the legal field, so she loved the black-and-white of the law, and she loved the Constitution, so that meant we loved it too.

Amongst the historical passages, we also were tasked with delving into the specifics of African-American history. I was partial to Martin Luther King, Sojourner Truth, and Harriet Tubman; my sister loved Malcolm X and gravitated to the "any means necessary" adage. Throughout this time of summer book reports and home presentations for our mother, we came across the story of the Tuskegee Airmen. My sister was the one who discovered the epic tale, which I grew to love equally.

———»+++

Right before the 2008 Presidential Election, I was asked to write one of my very first commissions for Lt. Colonel Lee Archer of the Tuskegee Airmen. He was being honored at a Los Angeles-based flight museum. I was still very new to the business of writing for a theme, but I was eager to reach back into my childhood memories and book reports. I eagerly accepted the commission and began to research. The sepia tone photographs I had Googled felt nostalgic. What I learned as an adult about the Airmen far exceeded what I remembered from my childhood. All at once, I felt a sense of pride and accomplishment for what these brave men had done, in a time when fellow soldiers didn't trust them because of their skin pigment. The Airmen continuously laid their lives on the line in battle and often flew back home triumphant. The poem came naturally, the story was full of passion, and the Lt. Colonel was a valiant, easy subject to daydream about. I wished to be born in another time, to be swept off my poetic feet by a caramel-toned pilot. Yes, that would have been superb.

.../-—-/...

I recall telling my mother about the commission. She was still in shock from the decision I made to pursue this career, so I invited her to see me perform. I requested a table for her at the event, and she invited six or so people to attend. I thought to myself, "Don't blow this, Azure, your mom is going to be watching." Never mind the historic, debonair Lt. Colonel I had been researching. This would be a validation marker. This was before the Maria Shriver moment that would convince her I was onto something.

When the night of the performance arrived, I went ahead of schedule for microphone check, to prepare myself to perform in front of the only person who made me nervous, Octavia Robinson. I felt confident in the poem I had written and hope that I didn't blush when standing next to the Lt. Colonel during photographs. I was calm, for the most part.

The announcer called my name, and I proceeded to the stage to recite the poem that I started researching long before I had been given the commission. I remember panning the audience as I recited. I saw smiles, intrigue, focus, and Octavia. She was nodding slowly. She had made me recite the poem at least 10 times at home and even asked me to gesticulate a salute once I finished. She nodded with the downbeat and she knew the rhythm. No matter what she had said before this moment, I knew that she wanted me to succeed, even if that meant as a poet. This might have been the first time that I had taken a breath, thinking that maybe she isn't so mad that I quit my job.

I finished the poem, took a picture with the still

handsome, divinely aged Lt. Colonel Lee Archer (I blushed), and took my seat.

Octavia, in a manner that only she could perfect, leaned over to me at the table and said, "Az, did you forget a line? I think you forgot a line. It doesn't matter, great job!"

I had a few choices at this point. I thought, "Well, this can go one of two ways..." I may have forgotten a line, but that wasn't what got me the most. What I found fascinating about this moment was that she was listening to each word. She had memorized the poem, just like she memorized the Preamble. She was listening, even though I walked away from human resources, from stability, thrusting myself into the very life that she didn't want me to have.

That night, I felt a little like an airman myself, who made it back home, triumphant.

//-—-//

» » A SALUTE...

Commissioned by Tomorrow's Aeronautical Museum for Tuskegee Airmen Col. Lee Archer

....

As a poet, some days I have trouble
getting my pen to make contact with a
page
Today, I wonder what it would be like to
have courage unbound by thoughts of
a nation that used to disregard heroics
because of the color of a man's skin
You sirs, Ebony Majesty, "Schwarze
Vogelmenschen"
You are the poets, you are the "Red Tail
Angels" providing fighter coverage for
men who demanded segregation once
upon a time
You are aviation titans
Aeronautic pioneers soaring through
history's skyline
Battling Nazis & Fascism, in North African
skies and European borders
Only to return to hit racism full phalanx
back on American soil
Sirs, you are people, the heroes that keep
me inspired

I will always remember how you set aside
your bias for a nation that shunned your
existence
Before this world knew men like you, we
did not possess the propensity,
Let alone the "audacity of hope" in the
words of President Barack Obama
I was looking through your eyes on
Inauguration Day
Be aware that your unparalleled
selflessness has been instrumental in
making this election possible
We must do more than certificates and
congressional medals on the finest silk
ribbon
We must do more
I propose a toast, a prayer, a moment of
praise, a plane dedicated in each of your
names - A Salute
To the fallen 66 audacious aviators, I pray
for your everlasting peace and know that
we have come so far as a country, you are
applauded, exalted, and praised here in
this land
To the 33 POWs, know there were vigils
held every dusk and dawn praying for
your safety and return
To the 150 Airmen who gave their lives
on land to forever live in the sky, know
you are amongst the beautiful unbiased
constellations, you are diamonds in an
indigo quilt

To those of you still gracing this life with
poise, humble swagger,
and the gait befitting the warriors that
you are, this country thanks you

With these words,
I, a poet, salute you

--o--

SHAKESPEARE, WILLIAM SHAKESPEARE

» *Her name was Mrs. Van Dyk, I will never forget her —she was the person that introduced me to William Shakespeare.*

And oh boy, did teen angst never look the same to me again.

I was in 11th grade, she was my AP English teacher and we had approached the time of year for the poetry section, I was not obsessed with poetry yet, I loved to talk, but I had never witnessed spoken word, just Maya Angelou's angelic delivery of On the Pulse of Morning for Bill Clinton's Presidential inauguration. Secretly, I knew then that what she did was something I aspired to do. But that didn't fit it with the popular, with the superficial; it didn't fit with the me I was then. I should tell you that I was the center of my universe, and thought that I was the nucleus of everyone else around me. Those kinds of people aren't poets; they aren't good little sisters, and they aren't the daughters that mothers pray for.

I was she, impenetrable to anything that didn't involve climbing the social ladder and school was not about education, it was a place to establish ones reputation, learning was tertiary, activities was secondary. I had no intention of falling in love with learning, at least not out loud, not so anyone knew that I journaled furiously at home, and sometimes during study hall.

During class, Mrs. Van Dyk would have us read aloud, passages, stories, and other material that we were no doubt going to have to correspond about in APA format. When we got to Shakespeare I knew nothing about him, vaguely knew of him, had heard of Romeo and Juliet, but I knew not of the longing, hadn't experienced the exquisite description of unrequited, had not ever read of love amongst 2 people that were not supposed to be together. I didn't know about iambic pentameter and that its predictable rhyme would send me into a love of archaisms that wasn't safe.

Who knew that I would become unhinged so easily? That all it was going to take was 3 lines of the prologue, just a smattering of the introduction, and that would be it, that would be the shift internally that made me love books the way my mother had always wished for me. During the Shakespeare section of class I found myself reading ahead, completing the homework in record time, and intently pouring over the metaphor, dreaming of the simile, undoubtedly head over heels for Billy Shakes.

When playwright Christy Joy asked me to write her prologue for her one woman show, my immediate thought was of my beloved Billy, and how he adored a blank page and then filled it with the epic tragedy. I instantly remembered how a book made me cry and wish for corsets and apothecary solutions to transport me breathless. I was slightly panicked because a prologue is what literally set my artistic life into motion and placed a time sensitive clock on the lemming I had turned into for the sake of being popular. I was not certain that I could be this epic, that I could write a prologue to change a perspective of someone who never wanted to be an intellectual, of someone who believed that love had NOTHING to do with anything.

But as I often do, I said "sure, I'd love to." Knowing good and well, I didn't ever think I could match up to Mr. Shakespeare, he wrote from a place that I had never been, with intent and passion, and that kind of passion is a disease, an epidemic to end all other obsessions – I could only have wished to be so ill.

Albeit, I was excited, nervous, but excited to try my pen at this art form that I loved. I hadn't done musical theatre since college and it was the last time I could remember the theatre, the melodrama of it all, so this would be a welcome treat. I can remember sitting down with Christy – I asked her what the title of the play was and she stated very matter of fact that it was titled "The Table". Furthermore, she wanted me to write a prologue as the table. Just to be clear, I had already said yes, to writing as a 4-legged piece of furniture. There were no apothocaries here, no holy palms kiss, no archaisms. Suddenly, this became an assignment, I was not looking forward to this, and that I swear by the moon, the inconstant moon.

As I digested what she had asked of me, I shifted my perspective, I began to think back on my creative writing courses, the personification section to be exact. This should be easy I thought, I was to think as a table, and make it a prologue. But in the nook of my right brain I kept recalling Billy's catalog, and I couldn't seem to locate the sonnet or tragedy where Mr. Shakespeare write a prologue as a chair. Of course, this is what happens when you say yes all the time.

We laughed, and once I stopped making light of this commission, Christy took the time to explain the magnitude, the title and her request for me to take on the subject matter that I was making light of.

At first, I thought tables were ordinary, simple and nothing to write home about. I didn't see them as a cornerstone for family meetings, declaration signing or rubber cement for families that count on this structure to hold their unraveling union together. My mother never allowed us to eat in our rooms, it was never okay in our house to segregate oneself during a time that was meant for families. Great things happened at the very piece of furniture that I mocked, the last supper, signing of the governing documents, and dinner for a single parent and her 2 children.

Through conversation, through commission I discovered that tables were epic, as worthy as Romeo, as poignant as the dialogue of Juliet, as handsome as sonnets from a poet gone mad with passion. Billy Shakes would have said yes to this assignment too, I am almost sure of it.

//-—-//

PROLOGUE

Commissioned by Christy Joy

--o--

If I were a prologue, instinctively your search would begin before Genesis, seeing as that is indeed defined as the beginning. But I have always been an anomaly—never what you expect. In truth, if you were searching for me, you would need to double-dutch over the beginning and land in Exodus, prepositioned in 36 and 38. Yeah, I'd be resting in the tenth verse of the 37th chapter.

This would be an Acadian beginning to end a rooted conversation—it may start with a description of dimension—36 by 18 by 27. My foundation is solid.

This is not a fable or parable of indirect meaning. This is a story of a table. A meeting place, constructed to showcase the showbread, this was representative of Christ. God instructed that I be draped with only

purest gold, finest China, settings to
befit heaven. I am where Jesus pulled
in the closeness of followed men to
supper one last time. I am lasting.

But there more than likely isn't time
for you to listen to me.
These days, there is just dust orbiting
the rings of Princess House that
was used last three Easter's ago.
Grandfather, you always told the best
jokes—made grooves into soft oak
smile and knots around legs curl.
I know, I am making you run behind—
but it has been so long since your
palms have rested on my surface, it's
been so long since I've seen you.

Trying to get you to gather around for
more than a moment is comparable
to hit-and-run on Manchester in
Inglewood—nobody sticks around.
Seems like I'm always centered
between a couch and screen that
broadcasts false realities and lullabies
to give new mothers some peace—
I'm only good for Nike soles and
Hungry-Man trays. I would rather
someone just pull into me and rest
their adolescent elbows and share
Thanksgiving memories about what
they are grateful for when it isn't
November.

I am a surface, not a parable—these
are the rants of a table.

I used to be a hold for matrimony,
adhering husband to wife, sharing
intimacies about arduous days and
overnight-overtime infantile cries. But
these days, I'm always centered around
a meeting or adulterous activities.
Be that dimly lit corners of forbidden
cafes, restaurants in cities that claim
to anchor business trips. I miss trust.
I am full of vomit, Isaiah—too many
libations sans scripture—I hold only
flutes and stems of fermented grapes
and spirits that were never holy. It is
less devotional materials, more Trojan
wrappers from one-night stands.
I used to provide raw materials to
make a night stand, and it would hold
candlelight while folks read the good
words of the promised Kingdom.

As for the work place, I haven't seen
a physical staff in years, 'cause Skype
connects continents together and
everyone holds Geneva conventions
in their drivers' seats. I used to love
Tuesday mornings. I used to hold
coffee with no whip and pastries that
were days old.

I heard a math teacher once say that
he thought I was only for people

of good financial standing, 'cause
they never had dinner table talks in
the hood. I wanted to tell him that I
would have gladly taken refuge in his
mother's kitchen if he could promise
me a visit a least once a week. His
latchkey perspective brought me new
knots, from youth comes wisdom.

So what if I were Christ and what if I
invited you to pull up a seat—bench,
throne, stool, Boston rocker, Carver,
chaise, La-Z-Boy, or a Ladder-back—
take your pick. I wonder if you would
remove your lion pride and come
in your naked state, with all your
transgression in tow.

Christ told me to tell you that you are
welcome, transgressions and all. Don't
worry about your appearance. Jesus
used to tell me stories of the places
he found Christians, and though I've
stood silent, I wonder if you knew
that the barkeeps and I held the same
secrets.

But let's just pretend—come with me,
heave the same legs that walked you
away from me underneath my leafs,
and imagine your loved ones

and you actually told your husband
what you thought he would never find

out and you actually let your wife into
your world of staggering insecurities
and your mother and father actually
spoke the same language that you
claim to communicate in

and while we are at it, we will
just pretend that a kiss is a sacred
sacrament—that courting is more than
a fairytale tradition
that black fathers actually do raise
their children
that single mothers is not a sought-
after lifestyle
that there is no skin tone more
pleasing than the next
and that those who attend church
need as much prayer as those who
never cross the threshold

and we will pretend that I am not
enormously heartsick that I have to
deliver this message as an inanimate
object adorning your dining room,
kitchenette, bedside, great room,
just holding down the corners of
your travertine tile hoping someday
that I'd see more than the bottom of
magazines and junk mail catalogs that
you will never read

we will pretend that I am more than
this prologue, and that you will sit
still long enough to feel—remember

that God's word is stronger than a 140
character status update that you type
to encourage people to believe that
you are indeed still a believer, and
that you do not validate your walk by
the number of "thumbs up" on your
scripture post

we will just pretend you believe that
commandments can be followed and
that this walk can culminate each day
with a meal, with a discussion, and you
can just pretend to pull in all that you
love around me

come close—hold fast to my corners...

--o--

>> >> NOT A DISCLAIMER

············

Any person whom I have ever coached, any student who has ever taken my class, can testify to my next statement: Never start your performance with a disclaimer.

So that is not what this is.
Mainly because it is after you have read these back stories.
After you have peered into what has carved itself into a career for me.

Thank yous are in order, to every single person who has graced the threshold of my life. Your influence has left a stain, an imprint, an impression on my being, most often coming out of fingertips that kiss keys or set the occasional pen stroke to a blank page. Every letter I meant to write, every journal entry turned haiku, every Post-it note that ran out of blank real estate and turned into an emotional manifesto for the day, was because you bothered to get involved in the kaleidoscope of events that made my memories.

I appreciate each kind word, every thoughtful moment that you thought I'd never remember, every single "it was nothing," each missed call and voicemail in an attempt to connect again, all the silence of misinterpreted text messages and every second that you stood around listening to my response to the question of "how are you?" It made the whole part of me that you see today.

To those of you who look past the Facebook and Twitter timeline, past the public person, I thank you for not running off at the sight of me unveiled. Thank you for sticking around, praying for my success, and wishing me grace in this world that is unbending to impatient, tortured souls. I have been asked so many times what I will talk about once life stops throwing me curve balls. I suppose if that ever happened, if things end up like screened-in porches and ice tea in mason jars, sitting next to my oldest friends, rocking on the downbeat of the patina wind chime—I will just reminisce how your presence gave my life antique, how your essence gave my life wrinkles. The kind you don't want to disappear with make-up.

This job, this birthright of writing

emotions, translating fragments into a word that is spoken, is that of a dream.

Many thanks, for everything I don't have the courage to write, and forgiving my mistakes. Thank you for not giving up on me being a human, an impulsive, deeply sensitive human who begs poetry to take her back each time she tries to skirt her emotion under "I'm good" and "it's ok." Chances are I wasn't "fine" when you asked, and things could definitely stand to be better all the time. Thank you for asking anyway.

It has been real—and for that I am ever appreciative. I have not had a job in years, and I have no intention of applying for one any time soon. I am blessed beyond measure. If I had advice to give, I would tell you that you should jump. Today you should say yes. Every journey is different, different peaks and levels of success. But the feeling of reward when you finally give into thing that drives you is amazing. I know that anyone who has jumped and said "yes" would agree. I say do it, I say planning is good, but flexibility is better. In everything that you do, love. Make sure to encourage and help wherever you can. Remember that we are all human and making

mistakes is as easy, easy as breathing.
So don't take anything too seriously; I
cannot say there is worth in that.

Here is to doing what you love, and
saying "yes."

HOODIE. (BONUS POEM)

....

To anyone who has ever said they
loved me.
I'm sorry, for being too passionate
about loving you back and
reckless with the essential things
of responsibility, patience, over
generosity, and balance.

But, you got me, right along with the
others who came before you.

I have always worn my heart around
the whole top part of my body like a
Champion hoodie, hood up, strings
drawn, even if the weather called for
a tank top. This heart has always been
out. This heart has always been too big
to fit on a sleeve.

Boundaries were forced on me at
six. I grew up inside a white picket
fence 'cause my mom thought she
was keeping the world out, when she
really shoulda' been worried about
me getting to them. And I imagined
strolling in Manhattan, kissing a boy

from Brooklyn wearing a Yankee fitted and I could never cite a team member other than Derek Jeter. I was a fan of far places, aggression, rude natures that really were only honest, and of all things forbidden.

New York seemed like the perfect prescription for an Inland Empire native.

In a world where tragedy is Queen, Mayhem is king and Unfortunate is the heir to the throne, I'm telling you that it's cool to rock middle upper class, wear it like a humble badge and do your thing in the public school where the district doesn't call for private education. Your parents worked hard to give you the life you got, and you ain't gotta run home 'cause your friends get shot after dark. I say, that's chill, you should rock that, till the wheels fall off of it.

To anyone who ever felt like they didn't fit in, I feel you.

I hailed somewhere in the middle, no gun powder residue, privately schooled, but fell in love with hooligans as though they looked like Precious Moments figurines. I could always see the alchemy. Running with the popular made my transition from awkward to notable easy in high school. I learned the power of gossip, that residing in the main crew meant that you never walked without a sidekick, the art of entrance, the skill of the unnoticeable exit. I learned the demon of looking down on others— and I was only 15.

Then to enter college, feeling catapulted back to 7th grade, where no one knows your name, and you are now the last four of your social and student ID. Re-enter hoodie, whilst end of summer, when I had gotten used to superficial spaghetti straps.

I again was begging for the validation of popularity. But this time was different, this was where the poem was going to be born and individuality would separate me from the lemming I'd become. It was frightening, 'cause not fitting in felt worse that always being told I was overweight, and this was before anorexia and bulimia was a trend I could follow, there was no guide on how to effectively become a cutter on YouTube. Back then, it was just you. The tube was optional.

I survived though, found solace in the underdog, and we became best friends. Unbeknownst to us both, my sister began to don a cape—training to be my hero.

I burned through the habits I courted in high school, was punched in the face by my first love, ridden of innocence by a man who's name doesn't deserve to be in this poem, skipped class to meditate at Venice Beach, mentored a high school drop-out through spoken word, moved to Queens with two weeks notice, dreamed of Bangalore, been vulnerable in front of a crowd of 15,000 women, cried from the gossip of a 12-year-old girl, and sat in jail next to prostitute for 72 hours on the first day of a new year for not paying my traffic tickets. I couldn't afford my infractions.

Discovering, through it all, that God has never stopped interceding on my life.

Finding out that it is not advisable to consciously stroll in crosswalks in Bed Stuy, hoping for the unfortunate incident that will stop this heart, stop this hoodie from beating, for all the wrong things.

Painfully realizing that I have to guard this affection with everything I have

left, with every stanza that will ever
fall from these lips.

And that I will have to ask your
forgiveness for everything I will fail at
in the future.

To anyone who has ever loved me and
said so out loud.
This is an apology for my shortcomings.

. . //– - — »

Say "YES."

— — » +